The *Mathematica* Primer

This book is a short, focused introduction to *Mathematica,* the comprehensive software system for doing mathematics. Written for the beginning user, this engaging book contains an explanation of essential *Mathematica* commands, as well as the rich *Mathematica* interface for preparing polished technical documents.

Mathematica can be used to graph functions, solve equations, perform statistical tests, and much more. In addition, it incorporates word processing and desktop publishing features for combining mathematical computations with text and graphics and producing polished, integrated interactive documents. You can even use it to create documents and graphics for the Web. This book explains everything you need to know to begin using *Mathematica* to do all these things and more.

Written for *Mathematica* Version 3, this book can also be used with earlier versions of *Mathematica,* and intermediate and advanced users may even find useful information here, especially if they are making the switch to Version 3 from an earlier version.

Kevin R. Coombes, Brian R. Hunt, Ronald L. Lipsman, John E. Osborn, and Garrett J. Stuck are all faculty members of the Department of Mathematics at the University of Maryland at College Park. Together, they have previously cowritten *Differential Equations with Mathematica* and *Differential Equations with Maple,* both with John Wiley & Sons.

The *Mathematica* Primer

Kevin R. Coombes   Brian R. Hunt   Ronald L. Lipsman

John E. Osborn   Garrett J. Stuck

CAMBRIDGE
UNIVERSITY PRESS

PUBLISHED BY THE PRESS SYNDICATE OF THE UNIVERSITY OF CAMBRIDGE
The Pitt Building, Trumpington Street, Cambridge CB2 1RP, United Kingdom

CAMBRIDGE UNIVERSITY PRESS
The Edinburgh Building, Cambridge CB2 2RU, United Kingdom   http: //www.cup.cam.ac.uk
40 West 20th Street, New York, NY 10011–4211, USA   http: //www.cup.org
10 Stamford Road, Oakleigh, Melbourne 3166, Australia

First published 1998

Printed in the United States of America

Typeset in Century Schoolbook and Avant Garde, in TeX and *Mathematica*.

Library of Congress Cataloguing-in-Publication Data
The Mathematica primer / Kevin R. Coombes ... [et al.].
      p.   cm.
    Includes index.
    ISBN 0-521-63130-0 – ISBN 0-521-63715-5 (pbk.)
     1. Mathematica (Computer file). 2. Mathematics – Data
   processing. I. Coombes, Kevin Robert, 1955– .
QA76.95.M3884   1998   97-51989
510'.285'53042 – dc 21   CIP

*A catalogue record for this book is available from
the British Library*

ISBN 0 521 63130 0 hardback
ISBN 0 521 63715 5 paperback

Contents at a Glance

Contents

Preface

Mathematica is a system for doing
mathematics by computer.
— Stephen Wolfram

That statement encapsulates the vision of Stephen Wolfram, the developer of Mathematica. Mathematica 3 is an ambitious program. It contains hundreds of commands to do mathematics. You can use it to graph functions, solve equations, perform statistical tests, and do much more. In addition, it incorporates word processing and desktop publishing features that allow you to combine mathematical computations with text and graphics and produce a polished, integrated interactive document. You can add sound. You can animate the graphics. You can export Mathematica documents in the HyperText Markup Language (HTML) for use on the World Wide Web.

A program this ambitious contains many features and options. The nine items on the main menu bar of the latest release of Mathematica contain more than 375 items in cascading menus, in addition to the hundreds of commands for doing mathematics. The standard reference (Stephen Wolfram, *The Mathematica Book*, 3rd edition, Wolfram Media/Cambridge University Press, 1996) is more than 1400 pages long and describes only core Mathematica; a separate book is needed to describe the standard packages that accompany the program.

Mathematica is more than a fancy calculator; it is an extremely useful and versatile tool. Even if you only know a little about Mathematica, you can use it to accomplish wonderful things. The hard part, however, is figuring out which of the hundreds of menu items, hundreds of commands, and thousands of pages of documentation you need to look at to start using it quickly and effectively.

That's where we come in.

Why We Wrote This Book

The goal of this book is to get you started using Mathematica successfully and quickly. We point out the parts of Mathematica you need to know without overwhelming you with details. We help you avoid the rough spots. We give you examples of real uses of Mathematica that you can refer to when you're doing your own work. And we provide a handy reference to the most useful features of Mathematica. When you're finished reading this book, you will be able to use Mathematica effectively. You'll also be ready to explore more of Mathematica on your own.

You might not be a Mathematica expert when you finish this book, but you will be prepared to become one – if that's what you want. We figure you're probably more interested in being an expert at your own specialty, whether that's finance or physics or psychology or engineering. You want to use Mathematica the way we do, as a tool. This book is designed to help you become a proficient Mathematica user as quickly as possible, so you can get on with the business at hand.

Who Should Read This Book

Complete novices, occasional users who want to sharpen their skills, intermediate or experienced users who want to learn about the new features of Mathematica 3, and even experts who want to find out whether we know anything they don't.

You can read through this Primer to learn Mathematica on your own. If your employer (or your professor) has plopped you in front of a computer with Mathematica and told you to learn how to use it, then you'll find the book particularly useful. If you are teaching or taking a course in which you want to use Mathematica as a tool to explore another subject – whether in mathematics or science or engineering or business or statistics – this book will make a perfect supplement.

As mentioned, we wrote this Primer for use with Mathematica 3. If you plan to continue using Mathematica 2.2, however, you can still profit from this book. The material on Mathematica commands in Chapters 2, 4–6, and 8 applies to both versions. Only the description of the interface in Chapters 1, 3, and 7 is exclusive to Mathematica 3.

How This Book Is Organized

In writing, we used our experience to focus on providing important information as quickly as possible. It contains a short, focused introduction to

Mathematica. It contains practice problems (with complete solutions) so you can test your knowledge. There are several sample Notebooks showing you how Mathematica can be used in real-world applications and an entire chapter on troubleshooting.

The core of this book consists of about 80 pages: the section of Chapter 1 for the particular platform you're using, Chapters 2–4, and the beginning of Chapter 5. Read that much and you'll have a good grasp of the fundamentals of Mathematica. Read the rest – the remainder of the Graphics chapter as well as the chapters on Applications, the Web, Troubleshooting, and the Glossary – and you'll know enough to do a great deal with Mathematica. You'll also know how to use online resources to enhance your expertise.

Here is a detailed summary of the contents of the book.

Chapter 1, *Getting Started*, describes how to start Mathematica on three different platforms: Windows 95, Macintosh, and the X Window System. It tells you how to type your first Mathematica command, how to save a file, and how to print it.

Chapter 2, *Mathematica Basics*, shows you how to do elementary mathematics using Mathematica. This chapter contains the most essential Mathematica commands.

Practice Set A, *Algebra and Arithmetic*, contains some problems for practicing your newly acquired Mathematica skills. Solutions are presented at the end of the book.

Chapter 3, *Mathematica Notebooks*, contains an introduction to the Mathematica Notebook interface. This chapter is an introduction to the word processing and desktop publishing features of Mathematica. After reading this chapter, you'll have an idea of what Wolfram means by a "system for doing mathematics".

Chapter 4, *Beyond the Basics*, contains an explanation of the finer points that are essential for using Mathematica effectively.

Chapter 5, *Mathematica Graphics*, contains a more detailed look at many of the Mathematica commands for producing graphics.

Practice Set B, *Calculus and Graphics*, gives you another chance to practice what you've just learned. As before, complete solutions are provided at the end of the book.

Chapter 6, *Applications*, contains examples of how to solve real-world problems using Mathematica.

Chapter 7, *Mathematica and the Web*, gives tips on viewing and posting Mathematica Notebooks on the Web.

Chapter 8, *Troubleshooting*, is the place to turn when anything goes wrong. Many common problems can be resolved by reading (and rereading) the advice in this chapter.

Next, we have complete *Solutions to the Practice Sets*. The *Glossary* contains short descriptions (with examples) of many Mathematica commands and objects. Though not a complete reference, the Glossary is a handy guide to the most important features of Mathematica. Finally, there is a complete *Index*.

Conventions Used in This Book

We use distinct fonts to distinguish various entities. When new terms are first introduced, they are typeset in an *italic* font. Output from Mathematica is typeset in a `monospaced typewriter` font; commands that you type for interpretation by Mathematica are indicated by a **`boldface`** version of that font. These commands and responses are often displayed on separate lines as they would be in a Mathematica Notebook, as in the following example:

```
In[1]:=  abc + xyz

Out[1]=  abc + xyz
```

Selectable items on the program's menu bar are typeset in a **boldface** font. Labels such as the names of windows and buttons are quoted, in a "regular" font.

We use three special symbols throughout the book. Here they are together with their meanings.

☞ *Paragraphs like this one contain cross-references to other parts of the book that amplify a point under discussion.*

⇨ **Paragraphs like this one contain important notes. Our favorite is "Save your work frequently." Pay careful attention to these paragraphs.**

✓ Paragraphs like this one contain useful tips or point out features of interest in the surrounding landscape. You might not need to think carefully about them on the first reading, but they may draw your attention to some of the finer points of Mathematica if you go back to them later.

About the Authors

We are all mathematics professors at the University of Maryland, College Park. We have been using Mathematica since its first release in 1988. We have used Mathematica in our research, in our mathematics courses, for presentations and demonstrations, for production of graphics for books and for the Web, and even for our taxes. We hope you'll find Mathematica as useful as we do, and that this book will help you learn to use it quickly and effectively.

Chapter 1

Getting Started

In this chapter, we describe how to start Mathematica, and how to open, save, and print Mathematica files. These operations are aspects of the interface between Mathematica and the particular computer operating system that you are using. These instructions differ from the commands you will use when you do mathematics with Mathematica; we introduce those commands in the next chapter.

⇨ **This chapter has three parts, one each for Windows 95, for the Macintosh, and for the X Window System under UNIX. You need only read the part that applies to your computer.**

The systems we describe use window-based interfaces, which are manipulated using a keyboard and a mouse. Moving the mouse causes a small arrow (called a *cursor*) to move on the screen. To *click* on an object, place the cursor over the object and press the mouse button. If your mouse has more than one button, use the left one. To *double-click*, place the cursor and press the button twice in rapid succession. To *drag* an object, place the cursor over it, press the mouse button, hold it while you slide the object where you want it, and then release the mouse button. You can drag a window by its titlebar.

We assume that Mathematica is already installed on your computer. If you are using a networked computer, some of the features we describe may be different for your particular installation.

Mathematica in Windows 95

We assume that you know the basics of Windows 95. If you don't, then you can learn them by clicking the **Start** button in the lower left-hand corner of the screen, then selecting **Help**, and then "Tour: Ten Minutes to Using Windows" from the "Contents" page of the window that appears. Windows 95 has extensive online help that is accessible from the **Start** menu, and from most applications, including Mathematica.

1

Starting Mathematica

✓ The Mathematica program uses a lot of memory, so you might want to close other applications before starting Mathematica. Active programs appear as buttons on the taskbar along the bottom of the screen.

The location of Mathematica on your computer will depend on your particular installation, so you may have to hunt around to find it. Click on the **Start** button in the lower left-hand corner, and then look in the **Programs** submenu for **Mathematica 3.x**, where 3.x is the version of Mathematica installed on your machine. You want the application **Mathematica 3.x** rather than **Mathematica 3.x Kernel**. The Kernel application starts Mathematica with a command line interface rather than the Notebook interface.

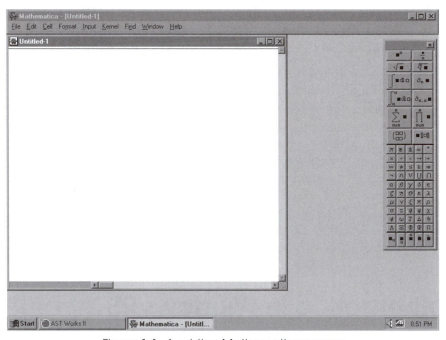

Figure 1-1: A pristine Mathematica screen

When you've found the Mathematica application, click on it. After a brief delay, Mathematica starts. There are three windows on the screen, as in Figure 1-1. The narrow horizontal bar at the top is the *menu bar*. The large blank window below it is a *Notebook*; the title shows that this Notebook is initially called "Untitled-1". The window on the right is a *palette* and is used for inserting formatted mathematical text or input into the Notebook.

☞ *Palettes will be discussed in Chapter 3.*

Typing in the Notebook

Click on the Notebook to make it active. When a window becomes active, its titlebar darkens. Now you can begin typing in the Notebook. Try typing **1+1**, and then hold down the SHIFT key and press ENTER. Pressing SHIFT+ENTER tells Mathematica to evaluate what you've typed. It will take some time for Mathematica to answer because it completes its loading process during the first calculation. Future responses to simple inputs should be nearly instantaneous.

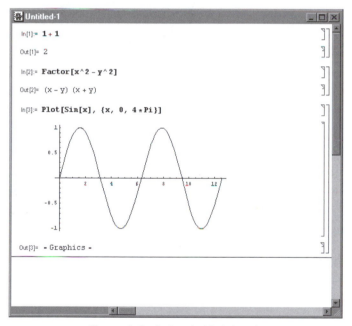

Figure 1-2: A simple Notebook

Type the input **Factor[x^2 - y^2]**, and press SHIFT+ENTER. Then type **Plot[Sin[x], {x, 0, 4 Pi}]**, and press SHIFT+ENTER. Your Notebook should look like Figure 1-2.

Saving Your Notebook

To save your Notebook to a disk, click on **File** in the menu bar. You will see the menu in Figure 1-3.

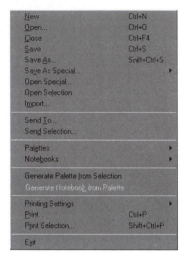

New	Ctrl+N
Open...	Ctrl+O
Close	Ctrl+F4
Save	Ctrl+S
Save As...	Shift+Ctrl+S
Save As Special...	▶
Open Special...	
Open Selection	
Import...	
Send To...	
Send Selection...	
Palettes	▶
Notebooks	▶
Generate Palette from Selection	
Generate Notebook from Palette	
Printing Settings	▶
Print	Ctrl+P
Print Selection...	Shift+Ctrl+P
Exit	

Figure 1-3: The File menu

Now select **Save** from the **File** menu. Figure 1-4 shows the "Save As" dialog box. Pressing the arrow button at the right end of the field labeled "Save in:" causes a list of drives and directories to appear. (The floppy drives are "A:" or "B:"; hard drives are "C:" or higher.) You can navigate this list to find the folder where you want to save the Notebook. After you find the proper folder, click in the box labeled "File name:" and type the name you'd like to use for the Notebook ("MyProject", for example). Then click "Save". A copy of the file will be saved on the disk, and the name of the Notebook will change from "Untitled-1" to the name you typed.

After a Notebook has a title, you can save additional changes by selecting **Save** from the **File** menu. Mathematica automatically remembers the file name. If you want to save the Notebook under a different name, you should use **Save As**.... If the computer you are using is attached to a network where you have an account, you may be able to save your Notebook on a central file server. Ask your system administrator for instructions.

⇨ **You should save your work frequently.**

Figure 1-4: The Save As dialog box

Opening a Previously Saved Notebook

To open a saved Notebook, click on **File** in the menu bar and then select **Open**.
Figure 1-5 shows the "Open" dialog box. You can navigate in this dialog box
by clicking on drives and/or folders until you see the name of the file you want.
After you select the file, its name appears in the region labeled "File name:".
Now click on the "Open" button.

Figure 1-5 : The Open dialog box

Mathematica saves Notebooks as files with the extension ".nb". (Older
versions of Mathematica saved Notebooks with the filename extension ".ma".)

To open a new blank Notebook, click on **New** in the **File** menu. You can
open and save as many Notebooks as you like, using a different name for each
one.

To close a Notebook without exiting Mathematica, make it active by clicking
in it or selecting its name from the **Window** menu. Then select **Close** from
the **File** menu. Or click on the "X" button in the upper right-hand corner of

the Notebook window. If the Notebook has changed since you last saved it, Mathematica will prompt you to save it.

Printing Your Notebook

Before printing a Notebook, make sure the Notebook you want to print is the active window. Then select **Print**... from the **File** menu.

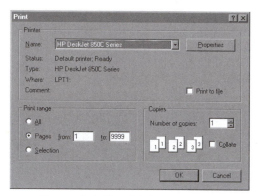

Figure 1-6: The Print dialog box

Figure 1-6 shows the "Print" dialog box. You can choose to print only a selected range of pages. You can do this by selecting "Pages", then typing the desired page numbers in the "from" and "to" boxes. If a PostScript printer driver has been installed, then you can also save the Notebook as a PostScript file by clicking the "Print to file" box. When you're finally ready to print, click on the "OK" button.

Online Help

Mathematica has an extensive online help mechanism. In fact, using only this book and the online help, you should be able to become quite proficient with Mathematica.

To access the online help, select **Help**... from the **Help** menu. By clicking in the window that appears, you can look up documentation for Mathematica commands. Figure 1-7 shows the documentation for the **NSolve** command, which we obtained by clicking "Numerical Computation", then "Equation Solving", and then "NSolve" in the Help Browser.

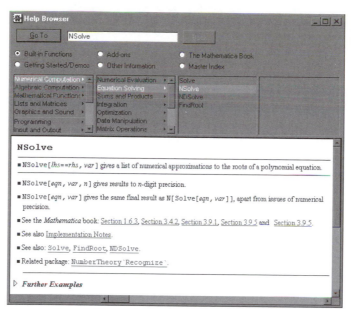

Figure 1-7: The Help Browser

☞ *See* Online Help *in Chapter 3 for more information on the Help Browser.*

Interrupting Calculations

If Mathematica is taking a long time to perform an operation and you want to stop it, you have two choices. You can click on **Kernel** in the menu bar, and then select **Abort Evaluation**. Or you can hold down the ALT key while pressing the PERIOD key. In either case, it may take some time for Mathematica to abort the calculation.

Ending the Mathematica Session

First verify that you have saved your work. Then select **Exit** from the **File** menu. Mathematica will give you one last chance to save any unsaved Notebooks.

☞ *Now you can proceed to Chapter 2, where we introduce the mathematical capabilities of Mathematica.*

Mathematica on a Macintosh

We assume that you know the basics of the Macintosh. If you don't, then you should look at the Macintosh "Tutorial" or the "Macintosh Guide"; both are accessible from the **Help** menu. The tutorial covers the basics of managing files and opening applications. You can also get a primitive kind of online help by turning on the **Show Balloons** option in the **Help** menu.

Starting Mathematica

✓ The Mathematica program uses a lot of memory, so you might want to close other applications before starting Mathematica. Use the menu attached to the Application icon in the upper right-hand corner of the screen to find out what programs are running.

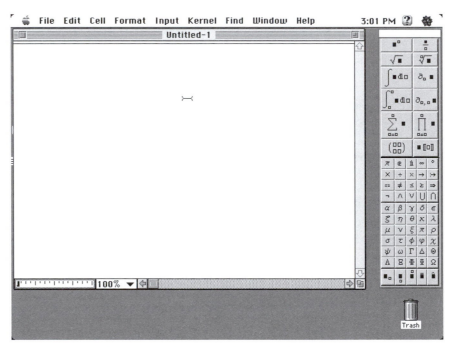

Figure 1-8: A pristine Mathematica screen

The icon for the Mathematica program is a stellated icosahedron with the name "Mathematica" printed beneath it. The location of this icon will depend on your particular machine, so you may have to hunt around to locate it. After you find the icon, double-click on it to open it. After a brief delay, your screen should look like Figure 1-8.

The narrow horizontal bar at the top of the screen is the *menu bar*. The large blank window below it is a *Notebook*; the title indicates that this Notebook is initially called "Untitled-1". The window on the right is a *palette* and is used for inserting formatted mathematical text or input into the Notebook.

☞ *Palettes will be discussed in Chapter 3.*

Typing in the Notebook

Click on the Notebook to make it active. When a window becomes active, the titlebar darkens. Now you can begin typing in the Notebook. Try typing **1+1**, and then hold down the SHIFT key and press RETURN. Pressing SHIFT+RETURN tells Mathematica to evaluate what you've typed. (If you prefer, you can use the ENTER key on the numeric keypad instead of SHIFT+RETURN.) It will take some time for Mathematica to answer because it completes its loading process during the first calculation. Future responses to simple inputs should be nearly instantaneous.

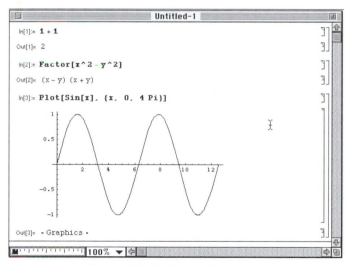

Figure 1-9: A simple Notebook

Now type the input `Factor[x^2 - y^2]`, and press SHIFT+RETURN. Then type `Plot[Sin[x], {x, 0, 4 Pi}]`, and press SHIFT+RETURN. Your Notebook should look like Figure 1-9.

Saving Your Notebook

To save your Notebook to a disk, click on **File** in the menu bar. Then select **Save** from the **File** menu. Select the "Desktop" button on the right-hand side of the dialog box. In the center of the dialog box, select the name of the drive where you want to save the file. Then click "Open". The dialog box will change to the "Save As" dialog box shown in Figure 1-10.

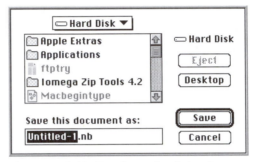

Figure 1-10: The Save As dialog box

There is a field labeled "Save this document as:". Type the name you'd like to use for the Notebook ("MyProject", for example), and then click "Save". A copy of the file will be saved on the disk. The name of the Notebook will change from "Untitled-1" to the name you typed.

After a Notebook has a title, you can save additional changes by selecting **Save** from the **File** menu. Mathematica automatically remembers where you want to save it. If the disk on which you originally saved the file is not in the drive, the Macintosh will report an error or will prompt you to insert the disk. In the latter case, you can get rid of the dialog box by inserting a disk or by holding down the COMMAND key and pressing the PERIOD key. (The COMMAND keys are located on either side of the space bar and have an apple and a cloverleaf symbol.) If you want to save the Notebook under a different name, you'll have to use **Save As**.... If the computer you are using is attached to a network where you have an account, you may be able to save your Notebook on a central file server. Ask your system administrator for instructions.

⇒ **You should save your work frequently.**

Opening a Previously Saved Notebook

To open a saved Notebook, click on **File** in the menu bar and then select **Open**. Figure 1-11 shows the "Open" dialog box. You can navigate in this dialog box by clicking on drives and/or folders until you find the file you want. After selecting the file, click the "Open" button.

Figure 1-11: The Open dialog box

Mathematica saves Notebooks as files with the extension ".nb". (Older versions of Mathematica saved Notebooks with the filename extension ".ma".)

To open a new blank Notebook, click on **New** in the **File** menu. You can open and save as many Notebooks as you like, using a different name for each one.

To close a Notebook without exiting Mathematica, make it active by clicking in it or selecting its name from the **Window** menu and then select **Close** from the **File** menu. Or click on the small box in the upper left-hand corner of the Notebook window. If the Notebook has changed since you last saved it, Mathematica will prompt you to save it.

Printing Your Notebook

Before printing a Notebook, make sure the Notebook you want to print is the active window. Then select **Print**... from the **File** menu.

Figure 1-12 shows the "Print" dialog box. You can choose to print a selected range of pages. You can do this by clicking next to "From", and then typing the desired page numbers in the "From" and "To" boxes. You can also save the Notebook as a PostScript file by choosing "File" in the box labeled "Destination". When you're ready to print, click on the "Print" button.

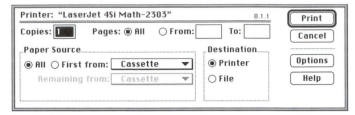

Figure 1-12: The Print dialog box

Online Help

Mathematica has an extensive online help mechanism. In fact, using only this book and the online help, you should be able to become quite proficient with Mathematica.

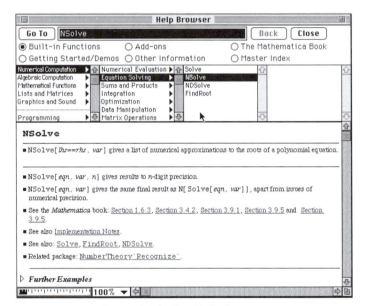

Figure 1-13: The Help Browser

To access the online help, select **Help**... from the **Help** menu. By clicking in the window that appears, you can look up documentation for Mathematica commands. Figure 1-13 shows the documentation for the **NSolve** command, which we obtained by clicking on "Numerical Computation", then "Equation Solving", and then "NSolve" in the Help Browser.

☞ *See* Online Help *in Chapter 3 for more information on the Help Browser.*

Interrupting Calculations

If Mathematica is taking a long time to perform an operation and you want to stop it, you have two choices. You can click on **Kernel** in the menu bar and then select **Abort Evaluation**. Or you can hold down the COMMAND key while pressing the PERIOD key. In either case, it may take some time for Mathematica to abort the calculation.

Ending the Mathematica Session

First verify that you have saved your work. Then select **Quit** from the **File** menu. Mathematica will give you one last chance to save any unsaved Notebooks.

☞ *Now you can proceed to Chapter 2, where we introduce the mathematical capabilities of Mathematica.*

Mathematica in the X Window System

We assume that you are using a computer running some version of the UNIX operating system together with the X Window System. We assume that you already have an account on the computer and know how to log on. The X Window System is highly customizable; you may need to ask your system administrator about the idiosyncrasies of your particular installation.

Starting Mathematica

Mathematica is often started by typing "mathematica" at the UNIX prompt. On your system, Mathematica might be started by clicking on a special menu button. Ask your system administrator for the precise command or start-up procedure. Whatever the procedure, after you start Mathematica, your screen should look like Figure 1-14.

There are two windows on the screen. The large blank window is a *Notebook*; the title shows that this Notebook is initially called "Untitled-1". The

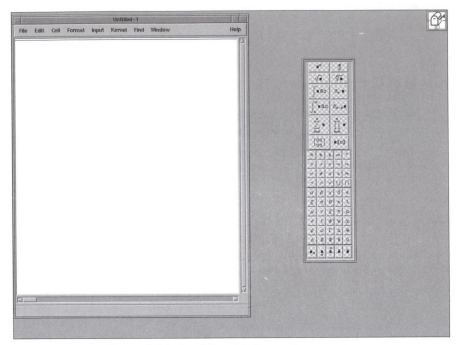

Figure 1-14: A pristine Mathematica screen

window on the right is a *palette* and is used for inserting formatted mathematical text or input into the Notebook.

☞ *Palettes will be discussed in Chapter 3.*

Typing in the Notebook

Click on the titlebar of the Notebook to make it active. When a window becomes active, the titlebar darkens. Now you can begin typing in the Notebook.
Try typing 1+1, and then hold down the SHIFT key and press ENTER. Pressing
SHIFT+ENTER tells Mathematica to evaluate what you've typed. (On some
systems, the ENTER key is labeled RETURN.) It will take some time for Mathematica to answer because it completes its loading process during the first
calculation. Future responses to simple inputs should be nearly instantaneous.

Type the input `Factor[x^2 - y^2]`, and press SHIFT+ENTER. Then type
`Plot[Sin[x], {x, 0, 4 Pi}]`, and press SHIFT+ENTER. Your Notebook
should look like Figure 1-15.

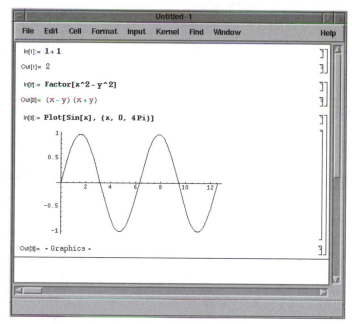

Figure 1-15: A simple Notebook

Saving Your Notebook

To save your Notebook, click on **File** in the menu bar. Then select **Save** from the **File** menu. Figure 1-16 shows the "Save As" dialog box.

The middle of this dialog box contains a list of directories and Mathematica Notebook files. Double-clicking on a directory opens the selected directory and produces a list of its subdirectories and files. After you have reached the directory in which you wish to save the Notebook, place the cursor at the end of the pathname in the "File name:" box and click. Then type the name you'd like to use for the Notebook ("MyProject", for example). Then click "OK". A copy of the Notebook will be saved, and the name of the Notebook will change from "Untitled-1" to the name you typed.

After a Notebook has a title, you can save further changes by simply selecting **Save** from the **File** menu. If you want to save the Notebook under a different name, you'll have to use **Save As**. . . .

⇨ **You should save your work frequently.**

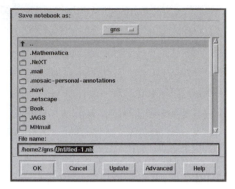

Figure 1-16: The Save As dialog box

Opening a Previously Saved Notebook

To open a saved Notebook, click on **File** in the menu bar and then select **Open**. Figure 1-17 shows the "Open" dialog box. You can move around the directory tree by double-clicking on directories until you see the file you want in the File region of the dialog box. Then double-click on the name of the file (or click on the name and select "OK").

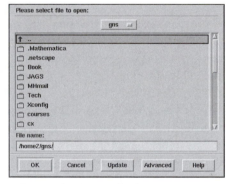

Figure 1-17: The Open dialog box

Mathematica saves Notebooks as files with the suffix ".nb". (Older versions of Mathematica saved Notebooks with the filename suffix ".ma".)

To open a new blank Notebook, click on **New** in the **File** menu. You can open and save as many Notebooks as you like, using a different name for each one.

To close a Notebook without exiting Mathematica, make it active by clicking in it and then select **Close** from the **File** menu. If the Notebook has changed since you last saved it, Mathematica will prompt you to save it.

Printing Your Notebook

Before printing a Notebook, make sure the Notebook you want to print is the active window. Then select **Print** from the **File** menu.

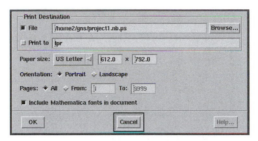

Figure 1-18: The Print dialog box

Figure 1-18 shows the "Print" dialog box. You can choose to print a selected range of pages. You can do this by clicking next to "From" and then typing the desired page numbers in the "From" and "To" boxes.

In the "Print Destination" field, there are buttons next to the words **File** and **Print to**. If you select **Print to**, your Notebook will be directed to the printer. If you select **File**, the Notebook will be saved as a PostScript file with the suffix ".ps". The default filename will be shown to the right of the word **File**. If you want to send the output to a PostScript file with a different name, you can click on "Browse..." to bring up a dialog box, or you can simply type the new filename. Finally, when you have everything as you want it, click on the "OK" button at the bottom of the dialog box.

Online Help

Mathematica has an extensive online help mechanism. In fact, using only this book and the online help you should be able to become quite proficient with Mathematica.

To access the online help, select **Help**... from the **Help** menu. By clicking in the window that appears, you can look up documentation for Mathematica commands. Figure 1-19 shows the documentation for the NSolve command,

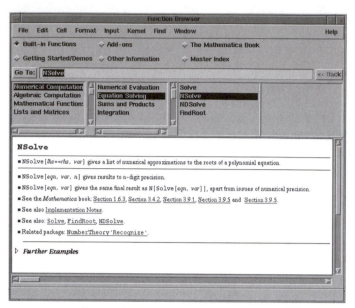

Figure 1-19: The Function Browser

which we obtained by clicking on "Numerical Computation", then "Equation Solving", and then "NSolve" in the Function Browser. We will also refer to this window as the Help Browser.

☞ *See* Online Help *in Chapter 3 for more information on the Help Browser.*

Interrupting Calculations

If Mathematica is taking a long time to perform an operation and you want to stop it, you have two choices. You can click on **Kernel** in the menu bar and then select **Abort Evaluation**. Or you can hold down the Mod1 key while pressing the PERIOD key. In either case, it may take some time for Mathematica to abort the calculation.

✓ To find out which key acts as "Mod1", go to the **Help** menu and then select **X Environment Information**.... In the dialog box that appears, look for the keys listed after "Mod1 KeySym". If that doesn't help, click on "Find keys and modifiers...". Then press keys until you find the one that makes "Mod1" appear next to "Modifiers". Keys near the space bar are a good guess.

Ending the Mathematica Session

First verify that you have saved your work. Then select **Quit** from the **File** menu. Mathematica will give you one last chance to save any unsaved Notebooks.

Chapter 2

Mathematica Basics

In this chapter, you will start learning how to use Mathematica to do mathematics. You should read this chapter at your computer, with Mathematica running. Try the commands in a Mathematica Notebook as you go along. Feel free to experiment with variants of the examples we present; the best way to find out how Mathematica responds to a command is to try it. For further practice, you can work the problems in Practice Set A.

☞ *The* Glossary *contains a synopsis of many Mathematica commands, options, functions, constants, and packages.*

Input and Output

You interact with Mathematica through Notebooks. A Notebook appears on your computer screen as a window containing text and graphics. A sample Notebook is shown in Figure 2-1.

Mathematica treats a Notebook as a complete document. In particular, Mathematica knows how to break the Notebook into pages to produce a finished, printed version of the Notebook. Every Notebook is divided into *cells* of different types. Cells are delineated by a bracket in the right-hand margin. In this section, we only discuss two types of cells: *Input cells* and *Output cells*. An Input cell is where you type expressions or commands for Mathematica to evaluate. An Output cell is where Mathematica gives its response.

☞ *We'll discuss the cell structure further in Chapter 3.*

Recall that you must press SHIFT+ENTER to tell Mathematica to evaluate what you've typed. The ENTER key by itself is a simple linefeed; it generates a new line but does not cause Mathematica to evaluate the input. It is useful if you want to group together several expressions or commands in a single Input cell.

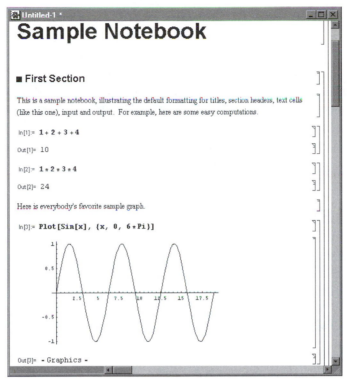

Figure 2-1: A Mathematica Notebook

✓ On some keyboards (typically on the Macintosh and some UNIX machines), the key in question is labeled RETURN. Furthermore, many keyboards contain another key, labeled ENTER, on the lower right of the numeric keypad. Pressing that key is equivalent to pressing SHIFT+ENTER.

As an example, try typing 2 + 3. It should appear at the top of the Notebook. To evaluate this expression, press SHIFT+ENTER.

✓ While Mathematica is working, it displays the word "Running..." at the top of the Notebook, and the bracket of the cell you evaluated is darkened. It will take some time for Mathematica to answer because it completes its loading process during the first calculation.

Your Notebook should now contain the following lines:

```
In[1]:=  2 + 3

Out[1]=  5
```

The symbol In[1]:= is an input label. An input label appears at the beginning of every Input cell after Mathematica has evaluated the cell. Inputs are numbered according to the order of evaluation. The output of the command is displayed in an Output cell and has the label Out[1]=. Mathematica formats the material in Output cells in mathematical notation.

Arithmetic

As we have just seen, you can use Mathematica to do arithmetic as you would a calculator. You can use "+" to add, "–" to subtract, "*" to multiply, "/" to divide, and "^" to exponentiate. For example,

```
In[2]:=  3*7 - 5^2 + 12/2

Out[2]=  2


In[3]:=  (5 + 2)(5 - 3)

Out[3]=  14
```

In the last example, we left out the * for multiplication. You can omit the * between delimiters, as in (5 + 2)(5 - 3), or between a number and a variable, for example, 3x. You can also use a space instead of *, even between numbers, as in 3 5. However, using a space for multiplication can easily lead to mistakes.

⇨ **We recommend that you avoid using a space for multiplication.**

Mathematica differs from a calculator in that it can do *exact* arithmetic. For example, it keeps track of fractions symbolically rather than using approximate decimal expansions, as a calculator would. Thus if you type 5/7, Mathematica will simply respond $\frac{5}{7}$. To force Mathematica to give a numerical (decimal) answer, type N[5/7].

```
In[4]:=  N[5/7]
```

Out[4]= 0.714286

✓ To get 15 digits instead of 6 in the answer, you would type N[5/7, 15]. (Try
  it. How would you get 1000 digits?)

You can also force Mathematica to use decimal approximations instead of
exact numbers by using a decimal point in the input. In fact, Mathematica
treats the decimal number "5.0" differently than the exact number "5". This
distinction is important because approximate, or floating point, arithmetic is
commonly faster than exact arithmetic, and floating point output is usually
less complicated.

Mathematica also does exact computations with roots, trigonometric functions, exponentials, *etc.*, as you can verify by comparing the expressions
Cos[5] and Cos[5.0], for example.

Algebra

Mathematica can also do algebra. For example,

```
In[5]:=  (x - y)(x - y)^2
```

Out[5]= $(x - y)^3$

```
In[6]:=  Expand[%]
```

Out[6]= $x^3 - 3x^2y + 3xy^2 - y^3$

```
In[7]:=  Factor[%]
```

Out[7]= $(x - y)^3$

☞ *The % symbol refers to the output of the previous command; see* Referring to
  Previous Output *later in this chapter.*

Although Mathematica makes minor simplifications to the expressions you
type, it does not make major changes unless you tell it to. The Expand
command told Mathematica to multiply out the expression, and the Factor
command forced Mathematica to restore it to factored form.

Mathematica has a `Simplify` command, which you can use to express a formula as simply as possible. At times this involves factoring; at other times, multiplying out. For example,

In[8]:= **Simplify[(x^3 - y^3)/(x - y)]**

Out[8]= $x^2 + xy + y^2$

In[9]:= **Simplify[(x^2 + x*y + y^2)(x^2 - x*y + y^2)]**

Out[9]= $x^4 + x^2y^2 + y^4$

⇒ **The asterisk between x and y on the last input line is necessary. Mathematica would have interpreted xy as a new variable, not as the product of x and y.**

Errors in Input

If you make an error when typing an input line, Mathematica will print an error message. For example, Figure 2-2 shows a Notebook containing a syntax error and Mathematica's response.

When Mathematica detects a syntax error, it prints a message describing its best guess at the source of the error. In this example, Mathematica tells you exactly what's wrong, and you can correct the input line and reevaluate it to obtain the desired output. (In Figure 2-2, we retyped the input line so that you could see both the error message and the correct output.)

⇒ **The most common errors on input lines are missing brackets and parentheses.**

Online Help

To view Mathematica's online documentation for a command, type `?command` in an Input cell. For example, you would type the input `?FindRoot` to get information on the `FindRoot` command. If you can't remember the name of a command, you can guess at all or part of the name of the command and use the wildcard character "*" to check for all commands containing the fragment

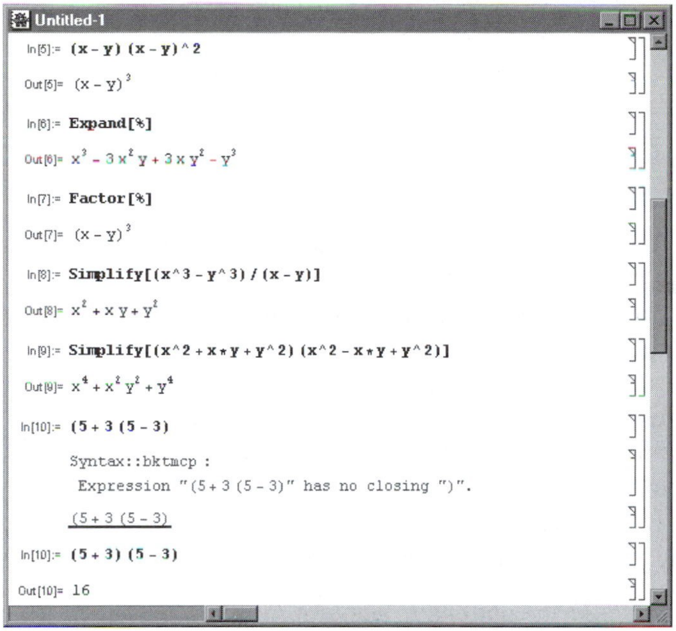

Figure 2-2: An error message

you typed. For example, to get a list of all Mathematica commands starting with the letter F, you would type `?F*`. Or if you want to factor a number, but don't know the name of the appropriate command, you could try typing `?*Factor*` to see a list of all the Mathematica commands containing the word "Factor".

☞ *You can use the Help Browser to get more information. We describe the Help Browser in Chapter 1 and Chapter 3.*

Options

Many Mathematica commands can be modified by using options. An option to a command is specified with the syntax `OptionName` $\rightarrow$ `OptionValue`. (The arrow is typed as a minus sign "-" followed by a greater than sign ">".) Here is an example.

```
In[10]:= Factor[Cos[x] + Cos[y]]
```

$$\text{Out}[10]= \text{Cos}[x] + \text{Cos}[y]$$

```
In[11]:= Factor[%, Trig -> True]
```

$$\text{Out}[11]= 2\text{Cos}\left[\frac{x}{2} - \frac{y}{2}\right]\text{Cos}\left[\frac{x}{2} + \frac{y}{2}\right]$$

The **Factor** command knows some trigonometric identities, but it will only use them if you include the option **Trig -> True**.

You can see a list of all possible options to a command, and their default values, by typing double question marks before the command name, as in **??FindRoot**, or by typing **Options[command]**, as in **Options[FindRoot]**. You can then get more information about an option by typing a question mark before the option name. For example, **?Direction** produces information about **Direction**, one of the options for the **Limit** command.

In most cases, you will not have to change the default values of options. In the graphing commands, however, many of the options are quite useful.

☞ *We describe options to the graphing commands in Chapter 5.*

Names and Assignments

In Mathematica, you use a single equal sign to assign values to a variable. For instance,

```
In[12]:= x = 7
```

$$\text{Out}[12]= 7$$

will give the variable **x** the value 7 from now on. Henceforth, whenever Mathematica sees the letter **x**, it will substitute the value 7.

```
In[13]:= x^2 - 2x*y + y
```

$$\text{Out}[13]= 49 - 13y$$

⇨ **To clear the value of the variable x, you can either type x = . or type Clear[x].**

You can make very general assignments.

```
In[14]:= Clear[x]
```

```
In[15]:= z = x^2 - 2x*y + y
```

Out[15]= $x^2 + y - 2xy$

```
In[16]:= z + 5y
```

Out[16]= $x^2 + 6y - 2xy$

```
In[17]:= y = 7
```

Out[17]= 7

```
In[18]:= z
```

Out[18]= $7 - 14x + x^2$

A variable name or function name can be any string of letters and digits, provided it begins with a letter (punctuation marks are not allowed). Mathematica distinguishes between uppercase and lowercase letters. You should choose distinctive names that are easy for you to remember, generally using lowercase letters. For example, you might use `cubicsol` as the name of the solution of a cubic equation.

You can also use the colon-equal sign (`:=`) to make an assignment. The colon-equal sign represents delayed assignment; *i.e.*, the right-hand side is not evaluated until the left-hand side is used in a later input. This is useful for defining functions.

☞ *Delayed assignment is described later in this chapter, and more fully in Chapter 4.*

⇨ **A common source of puzzling errors is the inadvertent reuse of previously defined variables.**

Mathematica never forgets your definitions unless instructed to do so. You can check on the current value of a variable by typing a question mark followed by the variable name. For example, to find the current value of the variable `z`, type `?z`.

Solving Equations

You write an equation in Mathematica using a double equal sign. You can solve equations involving variables with the `Solve` command or the `FindRoot` command. For example, to find the solutions of the equation $x^2 - 3x - 4 = 0$, you type

In[19]:= `Solve[x^2 - 3x - 4 == 0, x]`

Out[19]= $\{\{x \to -1\}, \{x \to 4\}\}$

There are two solutions, and Mathematica reports both of them.

The `Solve` command attempts to solve equations exactly. For many equations, particularly those involving transcendental functions like logarithms, exponentials, and trigonometric functions, it is impossible to find exact solutions. Even if found, exact solutions may be very complicated. The `FindRoot` command can often be used to find approximate solutions to such equations. The `FindRoot` command starts at a specified value of the variable and, using a numerical algorithm, looks for a solution nearby. For example, to find an approximate solution of the equation $e^x = 2x + 3$ that is close to $x = 2$, type

In[20]:= `FindRoot[Exp[x] == 2x + 3, {x, 2}]`

Out[20]= $\{x \to 1.92394\}$

Both `Solve` and `FindRoot` can also solve two or more equations in two or more unknowns.

In[21]:= `Solve[{r + s == 5, r - s == 2}, {r, s}]`

Out[21]= $\{\{r \to \dfrac{7}{2}, s \to \dfrac{3}{2}\}\}$

See the Help Browser for instructions on using `FindRoot` for multiple equations.

Built-in Functions

Mathematica has many built-in functions. These include `Sqrt`, `Cos`, `Sin`, `Tan`, `Log`, and `Exp`, as well as less familiar mathematical functions like `Gamma`, `Erf`, and `BesselJ`. Mathematica also has several built-in constants, including `Pi` (the number π), `I` (the complex number $i = \sqrt{-1}$), `E` (the base e of the natural logarithm), and `Infinity` (∞). Some examples:

```
In[22]:= Log[E^3]
```

$$Out[22]= 3$$

The `Log` function is the natural logarithm, called *ln* in many texts.

```
In[23]:= Sin[2Pi/3]
```

$$Out[23]= \frac{\sqrt{3}}{2}$$

To get numerical answers, you would use the `N` function. For example, you could type `N[Sin[2Pi/3]]`.

⇨ **You must use square brackets, not parentheses, for functions.**

For example, Mathematica would interpret the input `Log(E^3)` as a variable with the name "Log" times the number e^3.

✓ All of Mathematica's commands, built-in functions, and constants begin with a capital letter. To prevent confusion, use lowercase letters when you define variables or functions.

User-defined Functions and Expressions

You can define your own functions in Mathematica. In the following example, we define and evaluate a polynomial function at one point.

```
In[24]:= f[x_] := x^3 + 5x - 7
```

```
In[25]:= f[3]
```

$$Out[25]= 35$$

The underscore after the initial **x** means that **x** is a *dummy variable* in the definition, and the colon before the equals sign tells Mathematica not to evaluate the right-hand side until you actually use the function. It also suppresses the output.

You should distinguish Mathematica functions from ordinary expressions. For example, `x^3 + 5x - 7` is an expression. We can give a name to an expression, as follows:

```
In[26]:= g := x^3 + 5x - 7
```

Although this expression g looks very similar to the function f we defined earlier, it is actually quite different. The function is a rule for changing x into another quantity; the expression is just a quantity involving x. In particular, if you type g[3], you will not get the value of the expression at $x = 3$. (Try it to see what you do get!) In order to evaluate an expression at a particular point, you must use the replacement operator "/." and a transformation rule.

```
In[27]:= g /. x -> 3
```

```
Out[27]= 35
```

This input means, in the expression g, replace x by 3.

☞ *We discuss transformation rules and the replacement operator in* Transformation Rules *in Chapter 4.*

Referring to Previous Output

Mathematica assigns labels to every input and output line; this makes it easy for you to reuse previous results in later calculations. The % symbol refers to the last output; %% to the next-to-last output; and %n to the output labeled Out[n]. Here is an illustration:

```
In[28]:= 4 + 5
```

```
Out[28]= 9
```

```
In[29]:= %^2
```

```
Out[29]= 81
```

```
In[30]:= %%*3
```

```
Out[30]= 27
```

```
In[31]:= Sqrt[%28]
```

```
Out[31]= 3
```

A safer way to refer to previous output is to assign the output to a variable. For example, we could type:

```
In[32]:= diff = 6 - 2

Out[32]= 4


In[33]:= diff^2

Out[33]= 16
```

This is safer because the output in the preceding Output cell is not necessarily the output of the most recently evaluated command. If you have multiple Notebooks open, the most recent output may not even be in the current Notebook. Moreover, if you close and then reopen a Notebook, and then reevaluate the Notebook, the In/Out numbering will change; any references of the form %n will almost certainly be incorrect. Thus, you should assign a name to any output line that you expect to use later in a session, or in another session.

Lists and Tables

Mathematica allows you to arrange your data into lists. Lists can contain any kind of Mathematica object, including numbers, variables, functions, and equations. You enter a list in the form {x, y, z}, where x, y, and z are the individual elements of the list. In many cases, you can treat a list exactly like a single object. For example, you could type

```
In[34]:= w = {1, 2, 3, 4, 5}

Out[34]= {1, 2, 3, 4, 5}


In[35]:= w^3

Out[35]= {1, 8, 27, 64, 125}
```

In this example, we instructed Mathematica to cube the list w; it responded by cubing each element of the list. You can also add, multiply, subtract, and divide lists; plot lists of functions; and solve lists of equations.

✓ To find out whether a Mathematica command can be applied to a list, type ??command and look for the attribute Listable.

To extract the nth element from a list w, you would type either w[[n]] or Part[w, n]. The commands First and Last can be used to extract the first and last elements of a list, respectively, as in `First[w]`. A sublist of elements can be extracted from a list by specifying a list of positions. For example, typing `w[[{2, 4, 5}]]` or `Part[w, {2, 4, 5}]` produces a list consisting of the second, fourth, and fifth elements of the list `w`.

You use the `Join` command to combine lists. For example,

```
In[36]:= list1 = {a, b, c}
         list2 = {7, 8, 9}
         Join[list1, list2]
```

Out[36]= $\{a, b, c\}$

Out[37]= $\{7, 8, 9\}$

Out[38]= $\{a, b, c, 7, 8, 9\}$

In this example, we have used the ENTER key as a simple linefeed to enter three lines in a single Input cell.

Mathematica provides the `Table` command as an easy way to generate lists. Suppose, for example, that you want to generate a table of values of the function `f` (which we defined in In[24]) on the even integers from 0 to 10. You would type

```
In[39]:= Table[f[x], {x, 0, 10, 2}]
```

Out[39]= $\{-7, 11, 77, 239, 545, 1043\}$

In this command, `{x, 0, 10, 2}` specifies that `x` takes the values 0, 2, 4, 6, 8, 10. The "0" represents the starting value of `x`, "10" is the ending value, and "2" is the increment. The increment is optional; if you do not supply one, then the default increment is 1. This *iterator syntax* is common to many Mathematica commands.

The output of the `Table` command can be displayed in rows and columns by appending the command `//TableForm`, or by wrapping `TableForm[ ]` around the command. In the following example, we display a table of values with `x` in the first column and `f[x]` in the second column, where `x` is an integer between −1 and 3.

```
In[40]:= Table[{x, f[x]}, {x, -1, 3}] //TableForm
```

Out[40]//TableForm=

−1	−13
0	−7
1	−1
2	11
3	35

✓ Any Mathematica command that takes a single argument can be used at the end of an input statement in the suffix form `//command`. In addition to `TableForm` illustrated earlier, this syntax is especially useful with the commands `N` and `Simplify`.

On occasion, you may need to construct lists that depend on two or more parameters. To do this, you would use more than one parameter in the `Table` command. Here is an example, where we construct a list containing all fractions whose numerator is between 1 and 3 and whose denominator is between 2 and 4.

In[41]:= **Table[a/b, {a, 1, 3}, {b, 2, 4}]**

Out[41]= $\{\{\frac{1}{2}, \frac{1}{3}, \frac{1}{4}\}, \{1, \frac{2}{3}, \frac{1}{2}\}, \{\frac{3}{2}, 1, \frac{3}{4}\}\}$

The output contains two levels of braces, one for each parameter in the `Table` command. To remove the extra braces, you can type

In[42]:= **Flatten[%]**

Out[42]= $\{\frac{1}{2}, \frac{1}{3}, \frac{1}{4}, 1, \frac{2}{3}, \frac{1}{2}, \frac{3}{2}, 1, \frac{3}{4}\}$

Finally, to eliminate all duplicates from this list, you would type

In[43]:= **Union[%]**

Out[43]= $\{\frac{1}{4}, \frac{1}{3}, \frac{1}{2}, \frac{2}{3}, \frac{3}{4}, 1, \frac{3}{2}\}$

Vectors and Matrices

Vectors and matrices in Mathematica are represented by lists. A vector is an ordinary list consisting of the components of the vector. A rectangular matrix is specified as a list of lists: the sublists are the rows of the matrix. Thus to specify a 3×3 matrix we could type

In[44]:= **mat = {{1, 8, 2}, {4, 0, 0}, {8, 1, -1}}**

Out[44]= $\{\{1, 8, 2\}, \{4, 0, 0\}, \{8, 1, -1\}\}$

By analogy with `TableForm`, which displays lists in table format, the command `MatrixForm` displays lists of lists in matrix format.

In[45]:= **MatrixForm[mat]**

Out[45]//MatrixForm=
$$\begin{pmatrix} 1 & 8 & 2 \\ 4 & 0 & 0 \\ 8 & 1 & -1 \end{pmatrix}$$

✔ The output, as well as that of Out[40], is now a *formatted list*. Formatted lists are for display purposes only and cannot be used as input to other Mathematica commands.

☞ *Mathematica has many commands for manipulating matrices. You can read about them in the online help; some of them are illustrated in the* Fibonacci *section of Chapter 6.*

Graphics

The basic command for plotting an expression involving one variable is called **Plot**. Here is an example.

In[46]:= **Plot[4x^2 - x^4 + 2, {x, -3, 3}]**

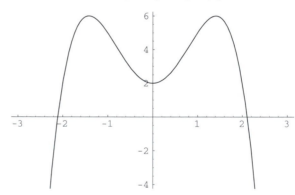

Out[46]= —Graphics—

The first argument to the **Plot** command is the expression to be plotted, and the second argument is a list, in this case **{x, -3, 3}**, specifying the independent variable, **x**, and its range, the interval $[-3, 3]$.

✔ Graphs can be misleading if you do not pay attention to the axes. For example, the input **Plot[4x^2 - x^4 - 6, {x, -3, 3}]** produces a graph that looks identical to the previous one, except that the horizontal axis is no longer the x-axis, but rather the horizontal line $y = -8$.

To produce a graph with a specified vertical range, use the `PlotRange` option. For example,

```
Plot[4x^2 - x^4 - 6, {x, -3, 3},
   PlotRange -> {1, 7}]
```

produces a graph with horizontal range $[-3, 3]$ and vertical range $[1, 7]$.

☞ *We describe more of Mathematica's graphics commands in Chapter 5.*

For now, we content ourselves with demonstrating how to plot a pair of expressions on the same graph. We enter the pair as a list and use the same plotting syntax.

```
In[47]:= Plot[{Exp[-x^2], x^4 - x^2}, {x, -1.5, 1.5}]
```

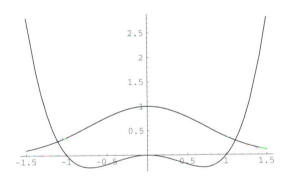

```
Out[47]= -Graphics-
```

Practice Set A

Algebra and Arithmetic

1. Compute:
   - (a) $7 + 4 + 2$
   - (b) 3^{321}
   - (c) e^2 and π to 25 digits
   - (d) the fractions $\frac{7}{5}$, $\frac{141}{100}$, and $\frac{707}{500}$, and determine which is the best approximation to $\sqrt{2}$.

2. Compute to 15 digits:
   - (a) $\cos(0.1)$
   - (b) $\ln(2)$
   - (c) $\arctan(1/2)$.

3. Factor the polynomial $x^4 - y^4$.

4. Use **FactorInteger** to find the prime factorization of 123456789. To interpret the result, read the help information on **FactorInteger**.

5. Use the **Simplify** command to simplify the following expressions:
   - (a) $1/\left(1 + 1/\left(1 + \frac{1}{x}\right)\right)$
   - (b) $\cos^2 x - \sin^2 x$.

6. Use the **Solve** command to solve the following equations:
   - (a) $8x + 3 = 0$
   - (b) $8x + 3.0 = 0$
   - (c) $ax^2 + bx + c = 0$ (solve for x)
   - (d) $2x + 3y = 7$, $3x - y = 2$ (solve for x and y)
   - (e) $x^2 y + 3x - 2y = 0$, $x + y = 3$ (solve for x and y).

7. Use **Plot**, with the **PlotRange** option if necessary, to graph the following:
   - (a) $y = 2x - 3$ for $-4 \le x \le 4$
   - (b) $y = x^2 - x + 2$ for $-4 \le x \le 4$
   - (c) $y = \sin x$ for $0 \le x \le 20\pi$
   - (d) $y = \tan(x/2)$ for $-\pi \le x \le \pi$, $-10 \le y \le 10$
   - (e) $y = e^{-x^2/2}$ and $y = x^4 - x^2$ for $-2 \le x \le 2$.

8. Consider the polynomial expression

$$x^6 - 21x^5 + 175x^4 - 735x^3 + 1624x^2 - 1764x + 720.$$

(a) Define a function $f(x)$ equal to the polynomial expression.
(b) Evaluate $f(0.5)$, $f(\sqrt{2})$, and $f(z^2)$.
(c) Make a table of the values of the function $f(x)$ at the sequence of points $x = 0.1, 0.2, \ldots, 1$.
(d) Factor the polynomial.
(e) Find the roots of the polynomial using the Solve command.
(f) Plot the polynomial for $0.9 \leq x \leq 6.1$.

Chapter 3

Mathematica Notebooks

In this chapter, we introduce important aspects of Mathematica's Notebook interface. We concentrate on the features that are essential to making effective use of Mathematica's symbolic, numerical, and graphical capabilities. In addition, we discuss formatting tools that allow you to integrate text into your Notebook and to create an attractive and polished document. For the most part, we describe the Windows 95 version of Mathematica 3; most features are similar on other platforms.

We use the following convention for referring to menu items: we type the name of the top-level menu, then a colon, then the name of the submenu (if applicable), and then the name of the item. For example, **Format : Style : Text** means the **Text** item of the **Style** submenu of the **Format** menu.

Keyboard Shortcuts

You may have noticed that some menu items have extra symbols on the right. These symbols represent a combination of keystrokes equivalent to the given menu item. For example, Figure 3-1 shows the **Find** menu, which can be used to search for (and replace) text in a Notebook. The **Find**... item is followed by "Ctrl+F". This is a *keyboard shortcut*. Holding down the CTRL (pronounced "control") key and pressing "f" has the same effect as selecting **Find**... with the mouse. Likewise, hitting the "F3" function key is equivalent to clicking on **Find Next**. These keyboard shortcuts are efficient alternatives to using the mouse. (Even though the keyboard shortcuts are displayed in the menus with capital letters, you should not press the SHIFT key unless explicitly instructed to, as with **Replace and Find Again** in Figure 3-1.)

⇨ **Keyboard shortcuts vary from one type of computer to another. You can learn the keyboard shortcuts by reading the menu items.**

✓ If you are using the Macintosh or the X Window System, see Chapter 1 for hints on locating special keys that are used in many keyboard shortcuts.

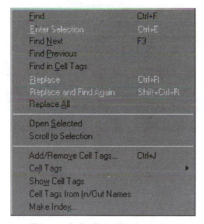

Figure 3-1: The Find menu

Online Help

As we've already indicated, Mathematica has extensive online help, which is accessible in several ways. First, you can get brief information about a Mathematica command by typing `?CommandName` or `??CommandName` in an Input cell. Second, you can get more detailed and cross-referenced information about Mathematica commands and the Notebook interface through the Help Browser. To do this, select **Help**: **Help**.... This opens the Help Browser, shown in Figure 3-2, which allows you to browse through a list of Mathematica commands and features.

Near the top of the Help Browser is a list of six database titles with small buttons next to them. (Your installation may not include all of these databases.) In Figure 3-2, the "Built-in Functions" database is selected. A list of top-level topics in this database is displayed in a box at the left edge of the window, beginning with "Numerical Computation". (Use the scroll bar on the right of the box to see the complete list.) Click on "Algebraic Computation", and the list of subtopics appears in the next box to the right. Select "Calculus", and a list of calculus commands appears. Finally, click on "Limit" to get the explanation of the `Limit` command shown in Figure 3-2.

✓ Another way to get to the same help text is to select "Built-in Functions", then type `Limit` in the box next to the "Go To" button, and finally press ENTER or click on "Go To".

The help text displayed in Figure 3-2 includes several underlined words

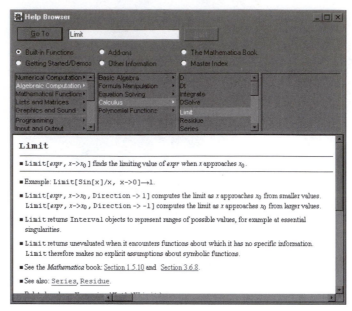

Figure 3-2: The Help Browser

and phrases. Each of these is a *link*, or cross-reference, to another part of the online help. You can click on a related command like `Series` to see its help text, or, if your installation of Mathematica includes *The Mathematica Book* online, then you can click on one of the section numbers to read a section of the book relevant to the `Limit` command.

Selecting other databases gives you access to additional information. For example, "Other Information" describes the Mathematica front end. The "Master Index" is an index to "Built-in Functions", "Add-ons", and "The Mathematica Book", but not the other databases. And in the "Add-ons" database, selecting "Standard Packages" yields information on packages of additional Mathematica commands.

☞ *See* Packages *in Chapter 4 for instructions on how to load packages.*

Some of the dialog boxes in Mathematica have a "Help" button that opens up the Help Browser and automatically displays information related to the given dialog box.

Cells

In Chapter 2, we observed that Mathematica Notebooks are organized into *cells*. Every cell has a particular type that determines how it is treated by Mathematica.

Types of Cells

A cell may be an Input cell (which Mathematica can evaluate), an Output cell (containing the result of a Mathematica computation), a Text cell, a Title cell, or a cell of any number of other types. See Figure 3-3 for common cell types and their default appearances. Each cell type is displayed in a particular font, with a particular formatting style. For example, Title cells are displayed in a large boldface font.

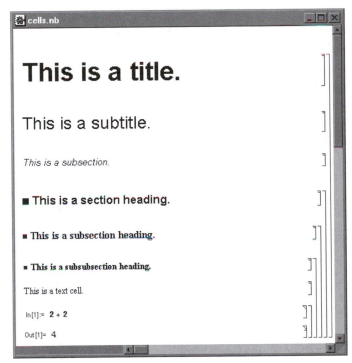

Figure 3-3: Common cell types

A cell is delineated by a bracket along the right edge of the Notebook. In

Figure 3-3, there are several levels of nested brackets. The leftmost bracket delimits an individual cell. Longer brackets to the right represent groups of cells.

☞ *See* Cell Hierarchy *later for more information on cell grouping.*

You can use Text cells to insert comments into your Notebooks. For example, if you want to make a graph and then interpret it, first type the appropriate plotting command in an Input cell. The graph appears in a Graphics cell, and then you can describe the graph in a Text cell below the graph.

To change the type of a cell, first select the cell by clicking on its bracket. The selected bracket will be highlighted. Then choose a cell type from the **Format:Style** menu. Many cell types have keyboard shortcuts. In Windows 95, these shortcuts are as follows:

ALT+1	Title	ALT+6	Subsubsection
ALT+2	Subtitle	ALT+7	Text
ALT+3	Subsubtitle	ALT+8	Small text
ALT+4	Section	ALT+9	Input
ALT+5	Subsection		

For example, to change a cell to a Text cell, click on its cell bracket, then press ALT+7.

✓ To check the type of a cell, select the cell by clicking on its bracket, then select the **Format:Style** menu. The type of the current cell will be marked in the menu of cell types.

Cursors

A cursor is a visible representation on the screen of the mouse's position. Mathematica uses different cursors to indicate different actions that are available in the Notebook. Move the mouse up and down through a variety of cells and watch the cursor change. We will describe the most important cursors. You can experiment with the others.

A horizontal I-bar cursor indicates that the mouse is at the boundary between two cells, or at the end of the Notebook. If you click the mouse button when the cursor is a horizontal I-bar, a horizontal line will be inserted into the Notebook. This horizontal line is a *cell insertion point*. In Figure 3-3, the cell insertion point is at the bottom of the Notebook.

To insert a new Input cell you simply start typing at the cell insertion point. If you want to insert a different type of cell, use the appropriate cell type menu item (or a keyboard shortcut) before typing. For example, to insert a new Text cell at the end of a Notebook you click at the end of the Notebook, select **Format** : **Style** : **Text** or its keyboard shortcut (ALT+7 in Windows 95), and then start typing.

A vertical I-bar cursor appears when the mouse is pointing at text that can be edited, *e.g.*, in an Input or Text cell. Clicking will create a thin vertical line that is called the *text insertion point*. The text insertion point indicates where you can add text by typing or delete text by using the backspace or delete key. When we refer later to the "insertion point" (*e.g.*, as a place to paste text from elsewhere), we mean either a cell insertion point or a text insertion point. You can use the arrow keys on the keyboard to move the insertion point around.

☞ *There are also several kinds of cursors that appear in* Graphics *cells. These are explained in* Graphics *later.*

Cell Hierarchy

One of the most useful features of the Notebook is the grouping of cells. An example is the automatic grouping of Input cells with Output cells. A cell group is delineated by an extra bracket along the right edge of the Notebook that surrounds one or more cell brackets. In Figure 3-3 you can see that the Input cell containing 2 + 2 and the corresponding Output cell are grouped together by a bracket that contains only those two cells.

Cells are automatically grouped according to a *cell hierarchy*. For example, if you create a Title cell at the top of your Notebook, there will be an extendible *grouping bracket* at the far right of the Notebook, which will enclose every other cell you create in the Notebook. If you then create a Section cell, a new grouping bracket will be created just inside the first grouping bracket. The new bracket will surround all successive cells until you create another Section cell. Similarly, Subsection and Subsubsection cells create additional nested grouping brackets. Again, see Figure 3-3.

Here is an example of how the cell hierarchy can be useful. When you start a document, create a Title cell at the top and type the title of the document. If your document has sections, then create a Section cell and type, for example, "Section 1". Now create Section 1 using Text cells, Input cells, Graphics cells, *etc*. All of these cells will be grouped together with a bracket along the right edge of the Notebook. When you are finished with Section 1, create a new Section cell and type "Section 2". A new grouping bracket for Section 2 will be created, and subsequent material in the Notebook will be grouped in this bracket until you add a new Section cell.

These grouping brackets can be used to manipulate blocks of cells. For example, if you click on the grouping bracket for Section 1 and then press SHIFT+ENTER, Mathematica will evaluate all the cells in this section, in order. If you double-click on the grouping bracket, the entire section will close up, and only the section title will be visible. A small triangle at the bottom of the grouping bracket indicates that a cell group is closed. To open the group, just double-click again on its bracket. For example, in Figure 3-4, Sections 1 and 3 and Subsection 2.A are closed, but Subsection 2.B is open and available for editing. In this way you can maintain a working notebook in outline form, opening only one section at a time for editing. If you experiment with this feature, you'll soon see how useful it is.

⇨ **When you print a Notebook, closed cell groups print in closed form.**

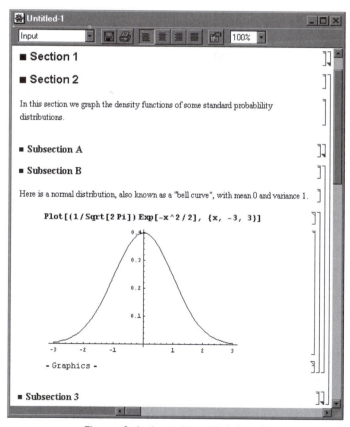

Figure 3-4: A working Notebook

Using Notebooks Effectively

In this section, we describe some features that are useful in managing and editing Notebooks.

Editing

The **Edit** menu contains the standard editing commands **Cut**, **Copy**, and **Paste**. You select text to cut or copy by moving the cursor to one end of the selection, pressing the mouse button, and holding it down as you move to the other end. The selected text will be highlighted. Release the mouse button when you have highlighted all the text you want to select. Then choose either **Edit : Cut** or **Edit : Copy**. Choosing **Cut** will delete the selected text and save a temporary copy in an invisible buffer called the *clipboard*. Choosing **Copy** will copy the selected text to the clipboard without deleting anything. To paste text that has been cut or copied, first move the cursor to the desired insertion point. Then click to set the insertion point and choose **Edit : Paste**.

You can select an entire cell or cell group by clicking on its bracket. The **Cut**, **Copy**, and **Paste** commands work for cells and cell groups. It is wise to save your Notebook before performing a substantial **Cut**.

✓ In Windows 95, the keyboard shortcuts for **Cut**, **Copy**, and **Paste** are CTRL+X, CTRL+C, and CTRL+V, respectively.

Manipulating Cells

Occasionally, you will want to divide or combine cells. To divide a cell, first set the insertion point at the place where you want the division to occur, then select **Cell : Divide Cell**. To merge several contiguous cells, first select the cells by dragging the cursor over a range of cell brackets, then select **Cell : Merge Cells**. The selected cells will merge, and the cell type of the new cell will be the type of the top cell. You probably should avoid merging formatted cells, such as Graphics and Output cells.

Selecting the menu item **Input : Copy Input from Above** places a copy of the contents of the preceding Input cell at the current insertion point. This is especially useful if you want to execute several variations of a single input expression. Likewise, **Input : Copy Output from Above** copies the preceding output.

Tool Bars

Mathematica offers various *tool bars* that can be displayed at the top of the Notebook. The most useful of these is the Edit Bar, which collects some of the most frequently used menu items in a convenient place. (The Edit Bar is not currently available in the X Window System.) You can enable the Edit Bar by selecting **Format**: **Show ToolBar**. The Edit Bar is displayed in the Notebook in Figure 3-4.

In the Edit Bar, the current cell type is displayed in the upper left, and clicking on the arrow to its right brings up a menu that you can use to change the cell type. To the right there are buttons to save and to print the Notebook, followed by four buttons that let you change the justification (left, centered, *etc.*) of the text in a given cell. Next there is a button to call up the Option Inspector, and finally a display of the current magnification.

Graphics

You can use the Notebook interface to manipulate graphics. Suppose, for example, that you have a Graphics cell containing the graph of a function. Click anywhere in the graph to select it. A frame will appear around the graph, as shown in Figure 3-4. You can move the graph by dragging it with the mouse. You can resize the graph by dragging one of the small squares along the edges of the frame. If you wish to return your Graphics cell to its default size and location, select the graph and choose **Cell**: **Make Standard Size**.

✓ Using the mouse, you can find the coordinates of a point on a graph. First select the graph. Then hold down the CTRL key (the COMMAND key on the Macintosh; the "Mod1" key in the X Window System) while moving the mouse around. The cursor will change to cross hairs, and the coordinates of the point in the middle of the cross hairs will appear at the bottom of the window.

Printing and Page Breaks

Mathematica distinguishes between two different *style environments* for a given Notebook: Working and Printout. The Working environment is what you see on your screen by default. The Printout environment is used by default when printing the Notebook. You can see what the Printout environment looks like by selecting it in the **Format**: **Screen Style Environment** menu.

If you want your Notebook to be printed in Working style, then you can select **Format** : **Printing Style Environment** : **Working**.

☞ *In* Font Styles *we discuss style sheets, which offer a variety of formatting options. Each style sheet has both a Working and a Printout environment. In addition, the Default style sheet supports Presentation and Condensed environments.*

When you send a Notebook to the printer, Mathematica automatically reformats Text and Input cells to fit the margins and breaks the Notebook into pages. You can inspect and adjust the page breaks before printing. To do this, select **Format** : **Show Page Breaks**. The display will switch to the current Printing Style Environment, and horizontal dashed lines will appear in the Notebook at places where Mathematica will produce a page break. You can inspect the page breaks to see if they are satisfactory.

The simplest way to fix bad page breaks is to add extra space at the bottom of a cell using the ENTER key. When you change one page break, all the remaining page breaks may change, so it may take some fine tuning to get the page breaks in acceptable places. When adjusting page breaks, it is good practice to start at the beginning of the Notebook and set the page breaks in succession as you step through it. When you're completely satisfied, then you can print the Notebook.

✓ If page breaks are displayed, then as you scroll through the Notebook, the page numbers will appear at the bottom of the window. This helps you to print selected pages of the Notebook as described in Chapter 1.

✓ It may be best to turn off page breaks, by selecting **Format** : **Show Page Breaks** again, before creating new cells in the Notebook. As of this writing, the Windows 95 version of the program does not handle keyboard input in new cells correctly while page breaks are displayed.

There are a number of ways to customize the printing of Notebooks. To adjust the margins, select **File** : **Printing Settings** : **Printing Options**.... By selecting **File** : **Printing Settings** : **Headers and Footers**..., you can control what is printed at the top and bottom of each page. And in Windows 95, you can adjust options specific to your printer by selecting **File** : **Printing Settings** : **Page Setup**..., or by clicking on "Properties" in the **Print**... dialog box.

Mathematical Typing and Palettes

In this section, we describe how to insert mathematical symbols and notation into a Notebook, and how to use other typographical features of the Notebook interface.

Palettes

When you start Mathematica for the first time, there should be a narrow window, called a palette, containing mathematical symbols, as in Figure 3-5. If this palette does not appear automatically, select **File** : **Palettes** : **BasicInput** to see it. The BasicInput palette consists of buttons you can use to insert mathematical notation into your Notebook. There are three types of buttons:

- mathematical symbols
- Greek letters
- templates for common mathematical notations

Clicking on a button inserts the corresponding symbol, letter, or template into the Notebook.

You can select additional palettes from the **File** : **Palettes** menu. Among the most useful are the BasicCalculations palette, which contains templates and brief descriptions for common commands, and the CompleteCharacters palette, which contains a vast number of symbols.

✓ Mathematica keeps track of the palettes you have on your screen when you exit the program. It brings those palettes up automatically the next time you run the program. Thus if you look at a palette and decide you're not interested in it, you should close it before exiting Mathematica.

Using Templates

At the top of the BasicInput palette are several buttons containing *templates* for mathematical notation. These templates include small boxes, called *placeholder boxes*, where you might expect numbers and symbols to appear. To use a template, first click on it to make it appear in your Notebook. Then fill in the boxes in the Notebook. You can also select an expression and then click on the template, in which case the selected expression will appear in the darkened placeholder box, and you can proceed to fill in the other boxes.

For example, suppose the insertion point is in an Input cell and you click on the button at the upper right of the BasicInput palette. This button is the

Figure 3-5: The BasicInput palette

template for a fraction. A copy of the template will appear in your Notebook; the placeholder box for the numerator will be darkened. Whatever you type next will appear in place of that box. When you are done typing the numerator, hit the TAB key to move to the denominator. (You can also use the mouse to do this.) Then type the denominator. If you want Mathematica to evaluate the fraction you just typed, you can go ahead and hit SHIFT+ENTER. However, if you are done typing the denominator and want to type more input, then you must press CTRL+SPACE (hold down the CTRL key and hit the space bar) to exit the template or use the mouse or the arrow keys to move the insertion point away from the template.

There are templates for exponentiation, roots, differentiation, definite and indefinite integrals, sums, products, and matrices. Whether you use the templates or type the associated Mathematica commands depends on which you find easier to enter or how you prefer your Input cells to look. Output cells will look the same regardless of which input method you choose.

The templates in the BasicInput palette can be used to insert mathematical notation into a Text cell. You fill in the boxes in the same way as described earlier; in addition, the template is highlighted while you are entering input to a template. You should press CTRL+SPACE twice, or use the mouse or arrow keys, to leave the template and continue typing text. You can go back later and correct an entry in the template.

✓ As of this writing, using templates sometimes produces undesirable results. Under some circumstances, clicking on a template causes raw Mathematica code to appear instead of the appropriate symbols. Also, the indefinite integral template does not yet work properly in Text cells.

Mathematical Typing

All of the symbols available in palettes have keyboard shortcuts. To learn the keyboard shortcut for a symbol, open the CompleteCharacters palette, find the desired symbol, and position the cursor over it. Two keyboard shortcuts will appear at the bottom of the palette. The first, and more concise, consists of the escape key, labeled ESC, followed by some text that is descriptive of the symbol, then ESC again. For instance, to insert π into your Notebook you can press ESC-p-ESC.

✓ You can use these symbols in an Input cell. For instance, you can use Greek letters as variables.

You can type subscripts and superscripts using the templates at the top left and in the bottom row of the BasicInput palette. For example, to type x_1 into a Text cell, first click on the button at the lower left corner of the palette. Then type **x**, TAB, and 1. Then click with the mouse to the right of the highlighted rectangle and keep typing. You can do the same thing without moving your hands from the keyboard: type **x**, then CTRL+_, then 1, then CTRL+SPACE (or the right arrow key) twice and keep typing. (To press CTRL+_, hold down the CTRL key and hit the key with the hyphen and underscore characters on it; there is no need to use the SHIFT key.) For a superscript, use CTRL+6 instead. (The mnemonic for this keyboard shortcut is the caret (^) that appears above the 6 on most keyboards.)

✓ Fractions can also be entered directly from the keyboard. Type the numerator, then CTRL+/, then the denominator.

You can read more about mathematical typing by selecting "Other Information" in the Help Browser, then selecting "2D Expression Input".

Font Styles

There are many ways to change the style of some or all of the text in a given cell using commands from the **Format** menu. You can change the type, size, and color of the font; put text into bold or italics; *etc.* First select the appropriate text by dragging the cursor across it. If you want to change all of the text in a cell, click on its cell bracket. Then, for instance, you can select **Format**:**Face**:**Bold** to make the text bold.

You can also change the style of the entire Notebook by selecting an option from the **Format**:**Style Sheet** menu. Further, you can create your own custom style sheet by selecting **Format**:**Edit Style Sheet**.... For more information, see "Edit Style Sheet..." in the "Other Information" section of the Help Browser.

Polishing a Document

Mathematica can be used to prepare polished documents, whether for a publication, a presentation, a Web page, or a solution to a homework assignment. When polishing a Notebook, make sure to delete material that is not relevant to the final document (typing errors, trial calculations, *etc.*). Interpretive text should appear in a logical place relative to the Mathematica output.

⇨ **Make sure that Input cells are reevaluated after they are edited.**

Failure to do so can result in Input and Output cells that are incompatible; *i.e.*, output that was not generated by the input directly above it. This is confusing and misleading to anyone reading the Notebook.

Additional Features and the Kernel

To conclude this chapter we discuss some features that you may wish to use after you become more experienced with the Mathematica user interface.

Working with Multiple Notebooks

You can use the **File** menu to open more than one Notebook at a time. Select **New** to create a new untitled Notebook, or **Open** to open a previously saved Notebook. You can copy and paste between Notebooks.

⇨ **Any definitions of variables or functions that you make in one Notebook carry over to other open Notebooks. In particular, if you evaluate Input cells in two different Notebooks, you may get unexpected results.**

You can recognize the active Notebook by its darkened titlebar; whatever you type will go into that Notebook. To activate a Notebook, click anywhere in its window. (In the X Window System, you may have to click on its titlebar.) You can move a Notebook by dragging its titlebar. To close a Notebook without quitting Mathematica, select **File : Close**. If you try to close an unsaved Notebook, Mathematica will ask if you want to save it first.

Manipulating the Kernel

Sometimes you may want to start over with a clean Mathematica session. This might happen, for example, if you are having problems caused by previously defined variables or functions that you can't easily eradicate. Or you may simply want to double-check that your Notebook runs correctly in a fresh session before sharing it with somebody else. One way to solve these problems is to quit and restart the *kernel*. When you quit the kernel, all variable and function definitions stored in the underlying Mathematica process will be cleared, but your Notebooks will remain on the screen unchanged.

To quit the kernel, select **Kernel : Quit Kernel : Local**. (In some installations, you may be running a nonlocal kernel, in which case you will have to figure out the appropriate selection in the **Kernel : Quit Kernel** menu.) A dialog box will pop up asking you to confirm that you want to quit the kernel; click on the appropriate button to proceed.

The next time you hit SHIFT+ENTER, a new kernel will start, and after a slight delay you can keep working as before. The In/Out numbering will be initialized to 1. Another way to reset the line numbering, without quitting the kernel, is to type `$Line = 0`.

You can also type commands directly to the kernel, without using the Notebook interface. To do so, start the command line interface by selecting the "Mathematica 3.x Kernel" application, where 3.x is the version of Mathematica installed on your machine (in the X Window System, type "math").

Evaluating the Notebook

When you open a previously saved Notebook in a new Mathematica session, you must reevaluate Input cells containing definitions and assignments that you want the kernel to use in evaluating your subsequent input. If there are many cells you want to evaluate, it may be easiest to evaluate the entire Notebook. To do this, select **Kernel**:**Evaluation**:**Evaluate Notebook**. You may have to wait awhile for Mathematica to redo all the calculations. Note that the In/Out numbering will almost certainly differ from your previous sessions with the Notebook, so an expression like %17 may no longer refer to the appropriate output.

✓ Input cells that are being evaluated or pending evaluation have highlighted cell brackets. This allows you to monitor the kernel's progress when evaluating the entire Notebook or a group of cells. You can keep working, for instance, by editing Text cells or creating new Input cells, while you wait for evaluation to finish.

The Option Inspector

We have already described several ways to customize your Notebooks. Many other advanced features and options can be selected through the *Option Inspector*. To open the Option Inspector, select **Format**:**Option Inspector**... or **Edit**:**Preferences**.... To change an option, first select the scope of your change in the box next to "Show option values for" (in the X Window System, "Scope"). Then locate the option you want to change using the menus in the main window of the Option Inspector and change it by clicking on the button to the right of its present value. For more information, see "Option Inspector" in the "Other Information" section of the Help Browser.

Chapter 4

Beyond the Basics

In this chapter, we describe some of the finer points of Mathematica and review in more detail some of the concepts introduced in Chapter 2. We explore enough of Mathematica's internal structure to improve your ability to work with complicated expressions and commands. At the end of this chapter, we introduce some of the Mathematica commands for doing calculus.

Suppressing Output

Certain Mathematica commands produce superfluous output. For example, when you assign a value to a variable, Mathematica echoes the value in an Output cell. You can suppress the output of a command by putting a *semicolon* after the command. Here is an example.

```
In[1]:=  y = x + 7

Out[1]=  7 + x

In[2]:=  z = x + 7;

In[3]:=  z

Out[3]=  7 + x
```

The semicolon does not affect the way Mathematica processes the command internally, as you can see from its output for the value of **z**.

You can also use semicolons to separate a string of commands when you are interested only in the output of the final command (several examples appear later in the chapter). If you use a semicolon after a graphics command, it will not suppress the graphic, but it will suppress the superfluous Output cell that ordinarily follows a graphic.

You can limit the output of a command to approximately one line by appending the suffix //Short to a Mathematica command. For example,

In[4]:= **Expand[(a + b)^100] //Short**

Out[4]= $a^{100} + 100 \ a^{99} \ b + \ll 97 \gg +100 \ a \ b^{99} + b^{100}$

The expression $\ll 97 \gg$ indicates that 97 terms have been omitted in the short form of the expression.

Functions

You can use the assignment method to define a function in the same way that you assign values to variables. For example, to define $f(x)$ to be the cubic polynomial $x^3 + 3x^2 - 2$, type

In[5]:= **f[x_] = x^3 + 3x^2 - 2**

Out[5]= $-2 + 3x^2 + x^3$

Now **f** is the name of a function of one variable. The independent variable (in this case, **x**) is also called the *argument* of the function **f**. The whole point of defining a function of **x** is to be able to replace **x** by different numbers or expressions. In this sense, **x** is a dummy variable standing for all the potential values that we might want to put into the function.

⇨ **The argument of the function must be enclosed in square brackets. On the left-hand side of the equal sign, the name of the argument must be followed by an underscore.**

✓ You can also define functions of two or more variables. For example, you could define **g[u_, v_] = u^2 + v^2**.

You can evaluate a function with either a numeric or a symbolic argument:

In[6]:= **f[-2]**

Out[6]= 2

```
In[7]:=  f[v^2]
```

$$Out[7]= -2 + 3v^4 + v^6$$

The result of this evaluation is the expression $-2 + 3v^4 + v^6$. This is a subtle point: the symbol f is the name of a *function*; the symbol f[v] is the name of an *expression* involving v.

☞ *You might want to review* Functions and Expressions *in Chapter 2.*

You can also define a function with delayed evaluation by using the "colon-equal" sign instead of the equal sign. For example,

```
In[8]:=  f[x_]  := x^3 + 3x^2 - 2
```

Here is the difference between the two methods. In the first method (without the colon), the right-hand side of the definition is evaluated as soon as you make the definition. In the second method (with the colon), the right-hand side of the definition is evaluated only when you ask for a value of the function. You can see the difference in Mathematica's lack of output from the definition with the colon-equal, which indicates that Mathematica is holding the definition in reserve for evaluation at a later time.

Here is an example that illustrates the distinction.

```
In[9]:=  express = x^3 + 5
```

$$Out[9]= 5 + x^3$$

```
In[10]:=  g[x_]  = express
```

$$Out[10]= 5 + x^3$$

```
In[11]:=  h[x_]  := express
```

```
In[12]:=  g[-2]
```

$$Out[12]= -3$$

In[13]:= **h[-2]**

Out[13]= $5 + x^3$

Why are the results different? With the := notation, the right-hand side of the definition is not evaluated at the time the function is defined. Thus h is the function $h(x) = express$. Then, when we evaluate h at 2, Mathematica substitutes the argument (in this case 2) for x in the expression on the right-hand side, *then* evaluates the right-hand side. Since x does not appear explicitly as a variable on the right-hand side in the definition of h, the function we define this way is actually independent of x. Thus h has been defined to be a *constant* function that always returns the same value, the expression *express* (whose value is $x^3 + 5$). In particular, the dummy variable x used in the definition of h is unrelated to the variable named x that occurs in the expression *express*.

On the other hand, when a function is defined with =, the right-hand side is evaluated immediately. In the definition of g, the right-hand side is *express*, which evaluates to $x^3 + 5$, so g is the function $g(x) = x^3 + 5$.

✓ The point of this discussion is that the distinction between = and := can be important depending upon when you actually want evaluation to occur.

Clearing Values

One of the most common sources of errors in using Mathematica is forgetting about previous variable or function definitions. For example, suppose that you type the following input during the course of a Mathematica session:

In[14]:= **c = 7;**

After working for another thirty minutes, you try to define a function of two variables by typing

In[15]:= **g[x_, c_] = c*x;**
         g[2, 5]

Out[15]= 14

The answer should have been $2 * 5 = 10$. But the function **g[x, c]** is not really **c*x**. Because c was previously set to 7, **g[x, c]** has actually been defined as **7x**. This case is so simple that you would probably notice that **g** isn't what it should be. In a complicated expression, however, it is difficult to detect this type of error.

Fortunately, there is an easy way to prevent this problem: clear the value of a variable either before using it or immediately after using it. To continue with the example, you can prevent the error by typing

```
In[16]:= Clear[g, x, c]
         g[x_, c_] = c*x

Out[17]= cx
```

You can also prevent it by using := instead of =.

```
In[18]:= c = 7;
         g[x_, c_] := c*x;
         g[2, 5]

Out[18]= 10
```

Because we have used := to define this function, Mathematica does not evaluate the right-hand side until the function is invoked. Then it uses the value of the variable specified in the function call rather than the previously defined value. In the earlier example, Mathematica evaluates the right-hand expression immediately and substitutes, once and for all, the value 7 for c. For this reason, it is often safer to use := rather than = when defining functions.

✓ To find the current value of a function or variable, just type a question mark before the function or variable name. For example, typing ?f will reveal the current value or definition of f.

The **Remove** command is similar to the **Clear** command, except that the former removes not only values, but also names. Consider the following sequence of inputs:

```
In[19]:= ?s

         Information::not found: Symbol s not found.

In[20]:= s

Out[20]= s
```

In[21]:= **?s**

Global's

The first output indicates that the symbol **s** is completely unknown to Mathematica. Then we enter the input **s**, without assigning anything to **s**. The final output indicates that Mathematica has "learned" the name of the symbol **s**, even though it doesn't have a value. **Remove** will remove the name of the symbol.

In[22]:= **Remove[s]**

In[23]:= **?s**

Information::not found: Symbol s not found.

The mere existence of a name can cause problems in certain situations, most notably when using packages.

☞ See Packages *at the end of this chapter for more information.*

If you open several Notebooks in a single Mathematica session, the definitions you make in one Notebook will carry over to the other Notebooks. This happens because the same Mathematica process, or *kernel*, underlies all the Notebooks. This also explains why the In/Out numbering carries over from one Notebook to another in a single session. If you enter input in one Notebook and the input line is labeled In[n], then the next input line will be labeled In[n+1], even if it is in a different Notebook.

Transformation Rules

Earlier, you saw how to evaluate a function at different values of the independent variable. To accomplish the same thing with expressions, you must combine the replacement operator **/.** with a transformation rule. For example,

In[24]:= **(x^2 + 3) /. x -> 4**

Out[24]= 19

You use the arrow notation **x -> 4** to write a transformation rule. So, this input line means, in the expression $x^2 + 3$, replace x by 4.

You can use the replacement operator to substitute for one or more variables in an expression using one or more transformation rules. Here is another example:

```
In[25]:= (c/(a^2 - 3*b)) /. {a -> u, b -> v, c -> w}
```

$$\text{Out[25]} = \frac{w}{u^2 - 3v}$$

In general, Mathematica's various "solve" routines report the solutions in the form of transformation rules. For example, the two solutions of the simple quadratic equation $x^2 - 4 = 0$ are $x = 2$ and $x = -2$.

```
In[26]:= soln = Solve[x^2 - 4 == 0, x]
```

$$\text{Out[26]} = \{\{x \to -2\}, \{x \to 2\}\}$$

Mathematica responds with a list containing two transformation rules. (Since we intend to use this list later, we have named it **soln**.) As you can see, Mathematica does not report the two solutions in the form "$x = 2$" and "$x = -2$"; these two assignments would conflict with each other. In fact, Mathematica never assigns values to variables unless you specifically direct it to do so. By reporting its results as transformation rules, Mathematica avoids assigning values to variables.

We can use the transformation rules generated by the **Solve** command. First, we have to extract the transformation rules from the list. To use the transformation rule $x \to -2$ on the expression $x^3 - 5x$, we type

```
In[27]:= x^3 - 5x /. First[soln]
```

$$\text{Out[27]} = 2$$

To use the rule $x \to 2$, we type

```
In[28]:= x^3 - 5x /. Last[soln]
```

$$\text{Out[28]} = -2$$

✓ Instead of using **First[sol]** and **Last[sol]** to extract the solutions from the list, we could have typed **sol[[1]]** and **sol[[2]]**. What would you do if there were more than two solutions?

⇨ **Options to Mathematica commands are generally specified as transformation rules with the syntax Option -> Value. You should always place options inside the brackets that delineate the command.**

Equations vs. Assignments

Mathematica distinguishes an *equation* from an *assignment*. For example, u
== 11 is an equation, whereas u = 11 or u := 11 is an assignment. In the
following example, the difference between entering an equation and entering
an assignment is reflected in the output lines.

```
In[29]:= u == 11
```

Out[29]= u == 11

```
In[30]:= u = 11
```

Out[30]= 11

⇨ **An equation has no effect on the value of the variables in the equation. An assignment does change the value of a variable.**

You can even assign a name to an equation.

```
In[31]:= Clear[a, b, c, x];
         quadratic =  a*x^2 + b*x + c == 0
```

Out[31]= $c + bx + ax^2 == 0$

```
In[32]:= Solve[quadratic, x]
```

Out[32]= $\{\{x \to \dfrac{-b - \sqrt{b^2 - 4ac}}{2a}\}, \{x \to \dfrac{-b + \sqrt{b^2 - 4ac}}{2a}\}\}$

Complex Arithmetic

Mathematica does most of its computations using *complex numbers*; *i.e.*, numbers of the form $a + bi$, where $i = \sqrt{-1}$, and a and b are real numbers. The
complex number i is represented as I in Mathematica. Although you may
never have occasion to enter a complex number in a Mathematica session,
Mathematica often produces an answer involving a complex number. For
example, many polynomials have complex roots.

In[33]:= **Solve[x^2 + 2x + 2 == 0, x]**

Out[33]= $\{\{x \to -1 - I\}, \{x \to -1 + I\}\}$

Both roots of this quadratic equation are complex numbers, expressed in terms of the number i. Some common functions also return complex values for certain values of the argument.

In[34]:= **Log[-1]**

Out[34]= $I\pi$

You can use Mathematica to do computations involving complex numbers by entering numbers in the form **a + b*I**.

In[35]:= **(2 + 3 I)*(4 - I)**

Out[35]= $11 + 10I$

Complex arithmetic is a powerful and valuable feature. Even if you don't intend to use complex numbers, you should be alert to the possibility of complex-valued answers when evaluating Mathematica expressions.

Pure Functions

Mathematica provides a way to define functions without explicitly naming the independent variables. These are called *pure functions*. There are two ways to enter a pure function in Mathematica. As an example, here are the two ways to define the pure function that sends the independent variable x to the value $x^3 + 3x^2 - 2$.

In[36]:= **f1 = #^3 + 3#^2 - 2 &**

Out[36]= $-2 + 3\#1^2 + \#1^3 \,\&$

In[37]:= **f1[x]**

Out[37]= $-2 + 3x^2 + x^3$

In[38]:= **f2 = Function[x, x^3 + 3x^2 - 2]**

Out[38]= $\text{Function}[x, x^3 + 3x^2 - 2]$

In[39]:= **f2[3]**

Out[39]= 52

In the first notation, the number sign (**#**) stands for the unnamed variable, and the ampersand (**&**) indicates that the expression is a pure function.

Mathematica occasionally reports its answers in pure function form. For example, if **f** has been defined as it was in In[5] near the beginning of this chapter, then Mathematica reports the derivative in pure function form if you type

In[40]:= **f´**

Out[40]= $6\#1 + 3\#1^2$&

Mathematica puts the 1 after the number sign to indicate the first variable; pure functions of several variables would contain $\#1$, $\#2$, *etc*. In this case, however, you can avoid the pure function form by typing

In[41]:= **f´[x]**

Out[41]= $6x + 3x^2$

☞ *Pure functions are useful for setting the options in plotting commands. See* PlotVectorField *in Chapter 5.*

Packages

Mathematica is a system composed of several parts. The *interface*, or *front end*, is the part that reads input, displays output, and manipulates Notebooks. The computational engine, or *kernel*, is the part that actually evaluates the input. The core parts of Mathematica, which must always be available, are contained in the kernel. The rest of Mathematica consists of *packages*, which contain extra commands. To use a command from a package, you must tell Mathematica explicitly to load the package. For example, the **ImplicitPlot** command is part of the collection of **Graphics** packages and must be loaded explicitly before it can be used. To load this command, type

In[42]:= **<<Graphics`ImplicitPlot`**

(Note that the word **ImplicitPlot** is surrounded by *backward* quotes.)

✓ You can make available all the commands in the collection of **Graphics** packages by entering the input **<<Graphics`**. The individual commands aren't loaded until you actually use them, and you won't be able to access the online help with the **?** syntax until after you've used the command.

If you try to use a package command before loading it explicitly, Mathematica will not recognize the command. It will simply echo the input line in the output area. For example, if you tried to use the **InequalitySolve** command from the **Algebra`InequalitySolve`** package before loading the package, you would see the following:

In[43]:= **InequalitySolve[x^2 > 2, x]**

Out[43]= InequalitySolve[$x^2 > 2$, x]

If you then loaded the package, you would see the following:

In[44]:= **<<Algebra`InequalitySolve`**

    InequalitySolve::shdw: Symbol InequalitySolve Appears in
    multiple contexts {Algebra`InequalitySolve`, Global`};
    definitions in context Algebra`InequalitySolve` may
    shadow or be shadowed by other definitions.

If you do make this mistake, the only way to recover (besides quitting and restarting the kernel) is to type **Remove[command]** and then load the package properly. For example,

In[45]:= **Remove[InequalitySolve]**

In[46]:= **<<Algebra`InequalitySolve`**

In[47]:= **InequalitySolve[x^2 > 2, x]**

Out[47]= $x < -\sqrt{2} \,||\, x > \sqrt{2}$

✓ The double vertical bar in the preceding output is Mathematica's notation for "or", so the output means $x < -\sqrt{2}$ or $x > \sqrt{2}$.

Most of the commands you will need are part of the Mathematica kernel. You can find out about additional package commands by browsing through the packages using Mathematica's Help Browser. Click the "Add-Ons" box in the Help Browser, then click on "Standard Packages". Then by clicking on the various packages you can see a list of commands in the packages and get documentation for individual commands.

Doing Calculus with Mathematica

Mathematica has built-in commands for most of the computations of basic calculus.

Differentiation

Mathematica has two commands for differentiating. Use the D command to differentiate expressions.

```
In[48]:= Clear[f, x]
         f[x_] := x^3;
         D[f[x], x]
```

Out[49]= $3x^2$

The output of D is another expression. The syntax for second derivatives is D[g[x], {x, 2}] or D[g[x], x, x], and for nth derivatives, D[g[x], {x, n}]. The D command can also compute partial derivatives of expressions involving several variables, as in D[x^2*y, y], or D[Sin[x*y/z], x, y].

The second way to differentiate is to use the *prime operator*, which works on functions.

```
In[50]:= f´
```

Out[50]= $3\#1^2\&$

Note that f´ is reported in pure function form. The function f´ can also be evaluated at numerical or symbolic values, as in f´[2] or f´[x].

```
In[51]:= f´[x]
```

Out[51]= $3x^2$

Integration

Mathematica can compute definite and indefinite integrals. Here is an indefinite integral:

```
In[52]:= Integrate[x^2, x]
```

$$\text{Out[52]}= \frac{x^3}{3}$$

Note that Mathematica does not include a constant of integration; the output is a single antiderivative of the integrand.

And here is a definite integral:

```
In[53]:= Integrate[ArcSin[x], {x, 0, 1}]
```

$$\text{Out[53]}= -1 + \frac{\pi}{2}$$

Mathematica can also do multiple integrals. The following command computes the double integral $\int_0^\pi \int_0^{\sin x} (x^2 + y^2)\, dy\, dx$.

```
In[54]:= Integrate[x^2 + y^2, {x, 0, Pi}, {y, 0, Sin[x]}]
```

$$\text{Out[54]}= -\frac{32}{9} + \pi^2$$

In multiple integrals, the integrations are performed from right to left. So, in the preceding example, the first integration is with respect to y, and the second is with respect to x.

Limits

The **Limit** command can compute right- and left-handed limits and limits at infinity. For example, here is $\lim\limits_{x \to 0} \dfrac{\sin(x)}{x}$.

```
In[55]:= Limit[Sin[x]/x, x -> 0]
```

$$\text{Out[55]}= 1$$

The option **Direction -> -1** gives a limit from the right and is the default except for limits at infinity. **Direction -> 1** gives a limit from the left. For example:

```
In[56]:= Limit[Abs[x]/x, x -> 0, Direction -> 1]
```

$$\text{Out[56]}= -1$$

Limits at infinity can be computed using the notation **x -> Infinity**.

```
In[57]:= Limit[(x^4 + x^2 - 3)/(3x^4 - Log[x]),
           x -> Infinity]
```

$$\text{Out[57]} = \frac{1}{3}$$

Sums and Products

Finite or infinite sums and products can be computed with Mathematica's `Sum` and `Product` commands. For example, here is the telescoping sum

$$\sum_{i=1}^{n}(1/i - 1/(1+i)).$$

```
In[58]:= Sum[(1/i - 1/(i + 1)), {i, 1, n}]
```

$$\text{Out[58]} = \frac{n}{1+n}$$

Here are two ways of computing the product of the even numbers between 2 and 20:

```
In[59]:= Product[2i, {i, 1, 10}]
```

Out[59]= 3715891200

```
In[60]:= Product[i, {i, 2, 20, 2}]
```

Out[60]= 3715891200

In the second example, the final 2 in the list {i, 2, 20, 2} indicates that the index i should be evaluated in increments of 2.

The `Sum` and `Product` commands can also be used to compute infinite sums and products. For example, here is the sum of the infinite geometric series:

```
In[61]:= Sum[a^i, {i, 0, Infinity}]
```

$$\text{Out[61]} = \frac{1}{1-a}$$

Note, however, that the answer is incorrect for $|a| \geq 1$.

Taylor Series

The `Series` command can be used to generate Taylor series expansions of a specified order at a specified point. For example, to generate the Taylor series up to order 10 at 0 of the function $\sin x$, we enter:

In[62]:= **sinseries = Series[Sin[x], {x, 0, 10}]**

Out[62]= $x - \dfrac{x^3}{6} + \dfrac{x^5}{120} - \dfrac{x^7}{5040} + \dfrac{x^9}{362880} + O[x]^{11}$

The output of the **Series** command can be used in other Mathematica functions. For example:

In[63]:= **sinseries^2**

Out[63]= $x^2 - \dfrac{x^4}{3} + \dfrac{2\,x^6}{45} - \dfrac{x^8}{315} + \dfrac{2\,x^{10}}{14175} + O[x]^{12}$

The **Normal** command can be used to truncate the series to give a Taylor polynomial.

In[64]:= **Normal[sinseries]**

Out[64]= $x - \dfrac{x^3}{6} + \dfrac{x^5}{120} - \dfrac{x^7}{5040} + \dfrac{x^9}{362880}$

The **Series** command can also be used to do series expansions of functions of several variables, as well as of certain functions involving fractional or negative powers. It can also be used to do series expansions at infinity. Here are two more examples.

In[65]:= **Series[Exp[1/x^2], {x, Infinity, 6}]**

Out[65]= $1 + \left(\dfrac{1}{x}\right)^2 + \dfrac{1}{2}\left(\dfrac{1}{x}\right)^4 + \dfrac{1}{6}\left(\dfrac{1}{x}\right)^6 + O\left[\dfrac{1}{x}\right]^7$

In[66]:= **Series[Sin[Sqrt[x]]/x, {x, 0, 4}]**

Out[66]= $\dfrac{1}{\sqrt{x}} - \dfrac{\sqrt{x}}{6} + \dfrac{x^{3/2}}{120} + O[x]^{5/2}$

Chapter 5

Mathematica Graphics

In this chapter we describe Mathematica's graphics commands. We also describe some options that can be used with graphics commands. Many of these options are common to all the graphics commands, though we usually illustrate their use with only one command. You can always see the available options, together with their default values, by typing **??command**.

Pay careful attention to the type of Mathematica object each plotting command is designed to plot. For example, the **Plot** command plots expressions involving a single variable. On the other hand, **PlotVectorField** plots a list of two expressions involving two variables. If Mathematica produces an error message or an implausible plot when you enter a plotting command, check that you plotted the right kind of object for that particular command and that you used precisely the right syntax for that object and that command.

Plot

This is the basic plotting command; it plots an expression or list of expressions in one variable over a specified interval. For example,

```
In[1]:= plot1 = Plot[{Exp[x]Cos[x], x^3 - 4x + 3},
        {x, -3, 3}];
```

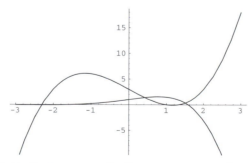

Here we have plotted $e^x \cos x$ and $x^3 - 4x + 3$ over the interval $[-3, 3]$. We have named this graph **plot1** for future reference.

✓ Recall that you can locate coordinates on your graphs using the mouse. This was explained in *Graphics* in Chapter 3.

The vertical range and the scales on both the horizontal and vertical ranges are selected by **Plot** to show the central features of the graph. The vertical range can be specified using the **PlotRange** option. This specification is often useful for focusing on an interesting feature of a graph. For example, the following command specifies the vertical range to be $[-6, 7]$:

```
In[2]:= plot2 = Plot[{Exp[x]Cos[x], x^3 - 4x + 3},
          {x, -3, 3}, PlotRange -> {-6, 7}];
```

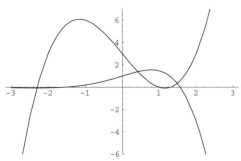

When Mathematica responds to the **Plot** command, it starts by evaluating the expression at 25 points in the specified interval. It then applies an algorithm to decide if the function is changing rapidly between points. If it is, then Mathematica samples more points. This is called *adaptive plotting*. Of course, all of this takes place behind the scenes; all you see is the final graph. You can force Mathematica to start with more or fewer sample points by using the option **PlotPoints** -> **n**. The default setting is $n = 25$. Higher settings will improve your graphs, but at the cost of an increase in computation time. The **PlotPoints** option can be used with all the plotting commands; the default setting varies.

✓ If your graph is jagged, or otherwise unsatisfactory, try increasing the value of **PlotPoints**.

Evaluate

Many of the plotting commands can be applied to lists of arguments, not just a single argument. For example, **Plot** was applied to a list of two expressions in the preceding section. You can pass a list of expressions to a plotting command using the **Table** command or some other Mathematica command. When you use a command inside a plotting routine, however, you must use **Evaluate** to force evaluation of the command. For example, you could type

```
In[3]:= Plot[Evaluate[Table[Sin[c*x], {c, 1, 3}]],
        {x, 0, 2Pi}];
```

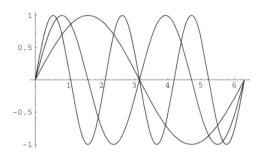

You can check that this command does not work if **Evaluate** is omitted.

✓ It is sometimes hard to tell whether **Evaluate** is necessary, but if you're having trouble getting a plot to work, you should try it.

ListPlot

ListPlot plots a list of points, given as coordinate pairs (x, y). You may give the list explicitly or generate it with the **Table** command. The option **PlotJoined** $->$ **True** causes **ListPlot** to connect the points with line segments.

```
In[4]:= plot3 = ListPlot[{{-3, -2}, {-2, 3}, {0.7, 8.3},
        {2, 1}, {3, 4}}, PlotJoined -> True];
```

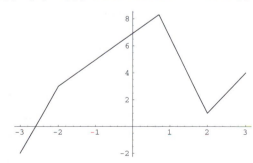

ListPlot has an alternative syntax. If you type

ListPlot[{y1, y2,..., yn}, PlotJoined -> True]

then Mathematica connects the points $(1, y_1), (2, y_2), \ldots, (n, y_n)$ with line segments.

ContourPlot

ContourPlot plots level curves, or contours, of an expression involving two variables; *i.e.*, contours or curves on which the expression is constant. By default, the contours correspond to a sequence of equally spaced constants. The contours are plotted on a rectangle, specified by giving a range for each variable in the expression. The following command plots a collection of curves of the form $x^2 + y^2 = constant$, on the rectangle $-6 \le x \le 6$, $-6 \le y \le 6$.

In[5]:= **plot4 = ContourPlot[x^2 + y^2, {x, -6, 6},**
          {y, -6, 6}];

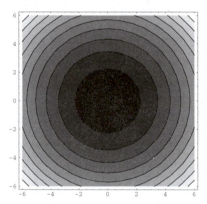

The shading in the plot signifies values of the expression: the larger the value, the lighter the color. The option **ContourShading -> False** turns off the shading. You can produce n contours with **Contours -> n**. You can produce contours at levels $a, b, \ldots$ with **Contours -> {a, b, ...}**.

☞ *See* Illuminating a Room *in Chapter 6 for an application of the* **ContourPlot** *command and the* **PlotRange** *and* **ContourShading** *options.*

ContourPlot works by computing the value of the expression at each point in a 15×15 grid of evenly spaced points in the specified rectangle. It then connects nearby points where the value of the expression is approximately the same. **ContourPlot** is not adaptive; *i.e.*, it does not try to refine the grid to produce a better plot. Thus you will often have to set the value of **PlotPoints** higher than the default value of 15 to get an acceptable plot.

Here is an example that uses some of the options we have discussed to graph the hyperbola $xy = 2$ on the rectangle $-10 \leq x \leq 10$, $-10 \leq y \leq 10$. Try it.

```
ContourPlot[x*y, {x, -10, 10}, {y, -10, 10},
  ContourShading -> False, Contours -> {2},
  PlotPoints -> 25]
```

DensityPlot

This command is similar to **ContourPlot** and has the same syntax (but different options). Given an expression involving two variables, and ranges for each of the variables, it produces a shading of the specified rectangle, with lighter colors corresponding to larger values of the expression. A sample is given in the Glossary.

ImplicitPlot

This command plots a curve defined by an equation in two variables. It is part of the **Graphics** package and is similar to the **ContourPlot** command with the option **Contours -> {c}**. A sample is given in the Glossary.

Show

The **Show** command superimposes several plots. We have named several of the plots so that we can use the **Show** command on them.

```
In[6]:= Show[plot1, plot3];
```

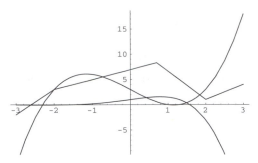

The order of the arguments in **Show** makes a difference. For example, suppose you have set **PlotRange** in the first plot. Then **Show** will use that **PlotRange** unless you specifically override it. Thus if you type **Show[plot2, plot3]**, then the top of **plot3** will be cut off because **PlotRange** was set to **{-6, 7}** in **plot2**. But if you type **Show[plot3, plot2]**, then **PlotRange** has the default setting, **Automatic**, that prevails in **plot3**.

Many of the options to the plotting commands can be set explicitly in **Show**. For example, we could type

> **Show[plot2, plot3, PlotRange -> {-5, 10}]**

to specify a vertical range of $[-5, 10]$; or we could type

> **Show[plot2, plot3, PlotRange -> {{0, 1}, {-5, 10}}]**

to specify the horizontal range to be $[0, 1]$ and the vertical range to be $[-5, 10]$.

The order of the arguments in **Show** has one additional effect. If you enter the command **Show[plot1, plot4]**, then part of **plot1** will be completely obscured by the shaded contour plot in **plot4**; this happens because **Show** first draws the curve in **plot1**, then draws the contour plot on top of it. If you enter **Show[plot4, plot1]**, then **Show** will draw the curve in **plot1** on top of the contour plot, and the curve will thus be more visible.

The horizontal range used by **Show** is the smallest range containing all the ranges of the specified plots. If you are planning to combine several plots with the **Show** command, you may want to make sure that the horizontal ranges of the graphs are comparable.

The command **Show[GraphicsArray[**array of plots**]]** displays an array of plots, arranged according to the structure of the array. For example,

> **Show[GraphicsArray[{plot1, plot2}]]**

displays the plots side by side;

> **Show[GraphicsArray[{{plot1}, {plot2}}]]**

displays the plots in a column; and

```
Show[GraphicsArray[{{plot1, plot2},
   {plot3, plot4}}]]
```

displays the plots in a 2 × 2 rectangular array.

ParametricPlot

ParametricPlot plots the curve traced out by a pair of expressions **{f[t], g[t]}** as the parameter **t** varies. For example,

```
In[7]:=  ParametricPlot[{Exp[-t/100] Sin[t],
         Exp[-t/100] Cos[t]}, {t, 0, 125},
         AspectRatio -> Automatic];
```

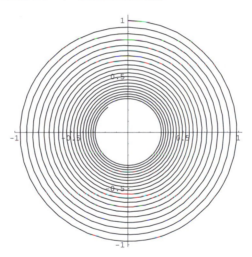

In this example, we have used the option **AspectRatio -> Automatic**. **AspectRatio** controls the height-to-width ratio for plots. The default value is the reciprocal of the Golden Ratio, approximately 0.618, which is classically considered to be pleasing to the eye. The **Automatic** option instructs Mathematica to use the same scale on both axes.

Here is another example of **ParametricPlot**, illustrating the use of the **Evaluate** command. Suppose we want to plot one lobe of the cycloid generated by rolling a circle of radius $1/4$. We define

```
In[8]:=  f[t_] := {(t - Sin[t])/4, (1 - Cos[t])/4};
```

Then we enter

```
In[9]:=  ParametricPlot[f[t], {t, 0, 2Pi}, AspectRatio ->
            Automatic];
```

ParametricPlot::ppcom: Function f[t] cannot be compiled;
     plotting will proceed with the uncompiled function.

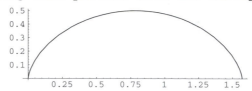

We could have prevented the warning message by typing

```
ParametricPlot[Evaluate[f[t]], {t, 0, 2Pi}].
```

PlotVectorField

PlotVectorField is used for plotting vector fields. This command is contained in the **Graphics`PlotField`** package. The components of the vector field are specified by two expressions involving two variables, as in the following example:

```
In[10]:=  <<Graphics`
            PlotVectorField[{x^2 + y, Sin[5*x*y]},
            {x, -1, 1}, {y, -1, 1}, Frame -> True];
```

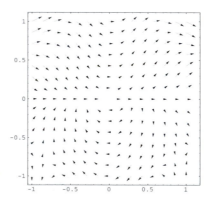

We have included the option **Frame** $->$ **True** in order to draw a box around the graph.

The **ScaleFunction** option can be used to rescale the length of vectors in the plot. The default setting, **ScaleFunction** $->$ **None**, causes the vector field to be displayed with vectors having length proportional to the magnitude of the actual vectors. The option **ScaleFunction** $->$ **(1&)** makes all the vectors the same length. The expression **1&** represents the pure function whose value is equal to 1.

Plot3D

The **Plot3D** command plots expressions involving two variables on a specified rectangular region. This command is a three-dimensional version of **Plot**. Unlike the **Plot** command, **Plot3D** will not plot a list of expressions.

```
In[11]:= Plot3D[x^2 - x*y^2, {x, -2, 2}, {y, -2, 2},
        AxesLabel -> {"x", "y", "z"}];
```

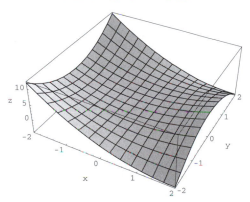

We have included the option **AxesLabel** $->$ **{"x", "y", "z"}** to label the axes, which are unlabeled by default.

The **Plot3D** command works by evaluating the expression on a 15×15 grid of evenly spaced points in the specified rectangular region. It then connects these grid point values with simple surfaces to obtain the graph of the expression. The plot is surrounded by a "bounding box", then projected onto a two-dimensional plane (your screen) from a particular viewpoint in space. Here is an example in which we increased the grid size to 25×25 and changed the viewpoint:

```
In[12]:= Plot3D[1/(x^2 + y^2), {x, -1, 1}, {y, -1, 1},
         PlotPoints -> 25, ViewPoint -> {1, -1, 2}];
```

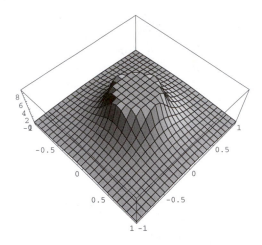

Changing the viewpoint has the same effect as rotating the bounding box in three-dimensional space and/or moving farther from or closer to the graph.

The preceding graph is truncated in the vertical z-direction. The function being plotted, $z = 1/(x^2 + y^2)$, approaches infinity near $(0, 0)$, but the vertical range in the graph is 0 to 8. By default, most Mathematica graphics commands will clip the graphic by excluding values of the expression that are extremely large in magnitude. The **Plot3D** command goes even further by filling in the clipped region; this is often misleading. You can turn off this filling with the option **ClipFill** $\rightarrow$ **None**. You can force Mathematica to show the full range of the plotted expression with the option **PlotRange** $\rightarrow$ **All**.

ParametricPlot3D

This command plots a parametrically defined three-dimensional curve or a parametrically defined three-dimensional surface. For example, the following command plots a torus:

```
In[13]:= ParametricPlot3D[{(2 + Cos[t])*Cos[u],
         (2 + Cos[t])*Sin[u], Sin[t]}, {t, 0, 2Pi},
         {u, 0, 2Pi}];
```

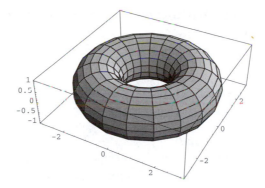

The next command plots a helix.

```
In[14]:= ParametricPlot3D[{Cos[t], Sin[t], t/4},
           {t, 0, 2Pi}];
```

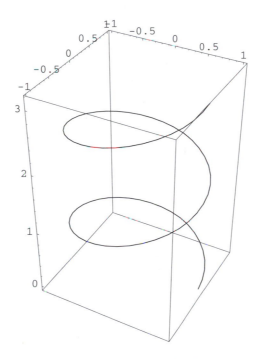

The arguments to **ParametricPlot3D** in the first example consist of a list of three functions of two variables, or parameters, giving the x, y, z coordinates of the points on the surface as functions of the parameters, and ranges for each of the two parameters. The arguments in the second example consist of a list of three functions of a single variable, or parameter, giving the x, y, z

coordinates of the points on the curve as a function of the parameter, and the range of the parameter.

Labeling and PlotStyles

There are several useful ways to enhance your plots. In this section we describe a few of them.

The **PlotLabel** option specifies a label for an entire plot. The **AxesLabel** option specifies labels for the axes. Here is an example.

```
In[15]:= Plot[Sin[t], {t, 0, 2Pi},  AxesLabel -> {"Time",
         "Amplitude"}, PlotLabel -> "Sine Wave"];
```

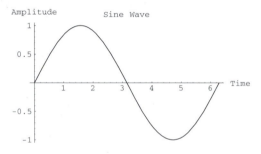

The labels must be enclosed in double quotes.

It is often useful to distinguish between two curves that are plotted together. Using the **PlotStyle** option, one can do this by varying the gray level or color of a curve, by varying the thickness of a curve, or by drawing a curve with dashes. The following command plots $\sin x$ in black and $\cos x$ in gray:

```
In[16]:= Plot[{Sin[x], Cos[x]}, {x, 0, 2Pi}, PlotStyle ->
         {GrayLevel[0], GrayLevel[0.7]}];
```

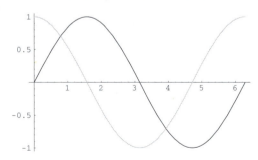

As an argument to **GrayLevel**, the number 0 represents black, 1 represents white, and numbers between 0 and 1 represent levels between black and white.

The command

```
Plot[{Sin[x], Cos[x]}, {x, 0, 2Pi}, PlotStyle ->
    {RGBColor[1, 0, 0], RGBColor[0, 1, 0]}]
```

plots $\sin x$ in red and $\cos x$ in green. **RGBColor[r, g, b]** specifies the red, green, and blue components of color, with r, g, b having values between 0 and 1. The value $r = 0$ specifies no red and values of r between 0 and 1 specify increasing levels of red. The other arguments in **RGBColor** work in the same way.

The following command plots $\sin x$ with the default solid curve of normal thickness (indicated by the empty list **{}**), $\cos x$ with a dashed curve, and $x(2\pi - x)/4$ with a thicker curve.

```
In[17]:= Plot[{Sin[x], Cos[x], x*(2Pi - x)/4},
        {x, 0, 2Pi}, PlotStyle ->  {{},
        Dashing[{0.03}], Thickness[0.008]}]
```

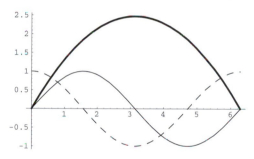

The number 0.03 in the **Dashing** directive specifies that the ratio of the length of the dashes to the total width of the graph is 0.03. The number 0.008 in the **Thickness** directive specifies that the ratio of the thickness of the curve to the total width of the graph is 0.008; the default setting (for two-dimensional graphics) is 0.004.

Animation

Mathematica can be used to produce animated graphics or "movies". Here is an example. We first make a table of plots. The following command makes a table of the graphs of $\cos x, \cos 1.2x, \ldots, \cos 5x$ on the interval $0 \leq x \leq 2\pi$:

```
Table[Plot[Cos[n*x], {x, 0, 2Pi}, PlotRange ->
    {-1, 1}], {n, 1, 5, 0.2}]
```

Next double-click on the cell bracket for the entire group of plots. This causes the group to close, leaving only the first plot visible. Then click on **Cell**:**Animate Selected Graphics**. This causes the plots to be animated. The plots are displayed in their given order in rapid succesion: the first plot, the second plot, ..., the last plot, the first plot, and so on.

In the lower left-hand corner of the Notebook, six small buttons will appear; see Figure 5-1. Clicking on the buttons has various effects on the animation in progress. The rightmost button causes the animation to speed up. The second button from the right causes the animation to slow down. The third button from the right causes the animation to pause. The leftmost button causes the order of animation to be reversed. The third button from the left returns the animation to the original order. The second button from the left causes the animation to proceed through the plots in their given order, then through them in the reverse order, then in the original order, and so on.

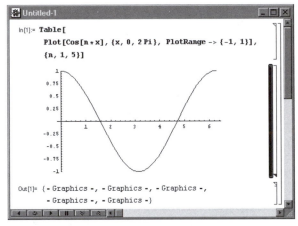

Figure 5-1: Animation buttons

Here is another example:

```
Table[Plot[{x^2, 1 + (x - 1)*(2 + h)}, {x, 0, 2},
  PlotRange -> {-2, 4}, AspectRatio -> Automatic],
  {h, 0.95, 0.05, -0.05}]
```

This command plots the curve $f(x) = x^2$ and the secant lines joining the points $(1, 1)$ and $(1 + h, f(1 + h))$ for several values of h. The animation shows these secant lines converging to the tangent line to the curve at the point $(1, 1)$.

Sound

If your computer is equipped for sound, Mathematica can produce sound. Here is an example:

```
Play[Cos[440Pi*t], {t, 0, 2}]
```

The **Play** command "plays" the given function. The function defines a waveform, and **Play** converts the waveform into sound; the values of the function give the relative amplitude of the sound as a function of the time **t** in seconds.

Miscellaneous Commands and Options

There are many options to the plotting commands besides the ones we have mentioned in this chapter, including **Axes**, **AxesOrigin**, **Boxed**, **Shading**, and **Ticks**. You can find out more about these options by referring to the Glossary or by typing **?** before the option name.

There are quite a few commands in the **Graphics** package that we have not described. Some of these are described in the Glossary, including **PieChart**, **BarChart**, **BarChart3D**, and **ContourPlot3D**. You can learn about other commands by clicking the "Add-ons" button in the Help Browser, then browsing through the **Graphics** package.

☞ *We use many of these commands and options in Chapter 6.*

Practice Set B

Calculus and Graphics

1. Plot the functions x^4 and 2^x on the same graph and determine how many times their graphs intersect. (*Hint*: You will probably have to make several plots, using intervals of various sizes, in order to find all the intersection points.) Now find the approximate values of the points of intersection using **FindRoot**.

2. Use **ContourPlot** to do the following:
   (a) Plot the level curves of the function $f(x, y) = 3y + y^3 - x^3$, in the region where x and y are between -1 and 1 (to get an idea of what the curves look like near the origin), and in some larger regions (to get the big picture).
   (b) A particular level curve of a function can be plotted using **ContourPlot** with the option **Contours** $\rightarrow$ **{c}**, where **c** is the value of the constant corresponding to the particular level curve to be plotted. Plot the curve $3y + y^3 - x^3 = 5$.
   (c) Plot the level curve of the function $f(x, y) = y \ln x + x \ln y$ that contains the point $(1, 1)$. (You will have to compute the appropriate value of **c** by evaluating $f(x, y)$ at the point $(1, 1)$. Note that the logarithm is only defined for positive values of x and y.)

3. Use **D** to find the derivatives of the following functions. If possible, simplify the answer.
   (a) $f(x) = 6x^3 - 5x^2 + 2x - 3$
   (b) $f(x) = \dfrac{2x - 1}{x^2 + 1}$
   (c) $f(x) = \sin(3x^2 + 2)$
   (d) $f(x) = \arcsin(2x + 3)$
   (e) $f(x) = \sqrt{1 + x^4}$
   (f) $f(x) = x^r$
   (g) $f(x) = \arctan(x^2 + 1)$.

4. Use **Limit** to evaluate the following limits:
   (a) $\lim\limits_{x \to 0} \dfrac{\sin x}{x}$

(b) $\lim\limits_{x \to -\pi} \dfrac{1 + \cos x}{x + \pi}$

(c) $\lim\limits_{x \to \infty} x^2 e^{-x}$

(d) $\lim\limits_{x \to 1^-} \dfrac{1}{x - 1}$

(e) $\lim\limits_{x \to 0^+} \sin\left(\dfrac{1}{x}\right)$.

5. Using the **Integrate** command, attempt to integrate the following functions. For the indefinite integrals, check the results by differentiating.

   (a) $\int_0^{\pi/2} \cos x \, dx$

   (b) $\int x \sin(x^2) \, dx$

   (c) $\int \sin(3x) \sqrt{1 - \cos(3x)} \, dx$

   (d) $\int x^2 \sqrt{x + 4} \, dx$

   (e) $\int_{-\infty}^{\infty} e^{-x^2} \, dx$.

6. Mathematica can also integrate functions numerically, producing an approximate, or numerical, answer. This is useful in cases where no elementary formula exists for an antiderivative, or where Mathematica cannot perform the symbolic integration. The command that does this is **NIntegrate**. It has the same syntax as **Integrate**. Find numerical values for the following integrals:

   (a) $\int_0^{\pi} e^{\sin x} \, dx$

   (b) $\int_0^1 \sqrt{x^3 + 1} \, dx$

   (c) $\int_{-\infty}^{\infty} e^{-x^2} \, dx$.

   For part (c), find the error in the numerical answer by comparing the numerical answer with the exact answer found in Problem 5.

7. Use **Plot3D** to plot the following surfaces:

   (a) $z = \sin x \sin y$ for $-10 \leq x \leq 10$ and $-10 \leq y \leq 10$. Use the option **PlotPoints** $\rightarrow$ **50** to give a smoother plot.

   (b) $z = (x^2 + y^2) \cos(x^2 + y^2)$ for $-1 \leq x \leq 1$ and $-1 \leq y \leq 1$.

8. This exercise illustrates three different ways to draw the unit sphere

$$x^2 + y^2 + z^2 = 1.$$

   (a) This sphere has the parametrization

   $$x = \sin \phi \cos \theta, y = \sin \phi \sin \theta, z = \cos \phi, \quad 0 \leq \phi \leq \pi, 0 \leq \theta \leq 2\pi.$$

   Use **ParametricPlot3D** to draw the sphere.

   (b) Use **ContourPlot3D** (in the **Graphics** package) to plot the sphere as a level surface of the function $f(x, y, z) = x^2 + y^2 + z^2$.

  (c) Use **Plot3D** to plot the upper hemisphere as the graph of the function
   $g(x,y) = \sqrt{1 - x^2 - y^2}$.

9. Use **Series** to find the Taylor polynomial of the indicated order n at the indicated point c for the following functions:
 (a) $f(x) = e^x, n = 7, c = 0$
 (b) $f(x) = \sin x, n = 5$ and $6, c = 0$
 (c) $f(x) = \sin x, n = 6, c = 2$
 (d) $f(x) = \tan x, n = 7, c = 0$
 (e) $f(x) = \ln x, n = 5, c = 1$
 (f) $f(x) = \mathrm{erf}(x), n = 9, c = 0$.

10. Use **Sum** to compute the following sums:
 (a) $\Sigma_{i=1}^{n} i^2$
 (b) $\Sigma_{i=0}^{n} r^i$
 (c) $\Sigma_{i=1}^{\infty} \dfrac{1}{i^2}$
 (d) $\Sigma_{i=0}^{\infty} \dfrac{x^i}{i!}$
 (e) $\Sigma_{i=-\infty}^{\infty} \dfrac{1}{(z-i)^2}$.

11. Use **Table** to make a table of the plots of the circles of radius $1/2$ centered at the points $(4,0)$, $(4\cos\pi/8, 4\sin\pi/8)$, $(4\cos\pi/4, 4\sin\pi/4)$, $(4\cos 3\pi/8, 4\sin 3\pi/8)$, ..., $(4\cos 15\pi/8, 4\sin 15\pi/8)$ on the circle of radius 4. Then animate this graphic by clicking on **Cell:Animate Selected Graphics**.

Chapter 6

Applications

In this chapter, we present examples showing you how to apply Mathematica to problems in several different disciplines. Each example is presented as a Mathematica Notebook, prepared using the "TutorialBook" style sheet. These Notebooks are illustrations of the kinds of polished, integrated interactive documents that you can create with Mathematica. The Notebooks are

- Illuminating a Room
- Mortgage Payments
- Cryptography
- Fibonacci Numbers
- Monte Carlo Simulation
- Population Dynamics
- Chemical Reactions
- The $360°$ Pendulum

As you will see, the Mathematica commands that we have already discussed in this book are useful in varied contexts. In the examples, we introduce additional commands that are particularly well-adapted to the applications. We have not explained all the commands that we use; you can learn about the new commands from the online help.

The Notebooks require different levels of mathematical background. *Illuminating a Room*, *Mortgage Payments*, and *Population Dynamics* use only high school mathematics. *Cryptography* uses some number theory; *Fibonacci Numbers*, some linear algebra; *Monte Carlo Simulation*, some statistics; *Chemical Reactions* and the *The $360°$ Pendulum*, some differential equations. Read the ones that interest you; even if you don't have the background for a particular example, you should be able to learn something about Mathematica from the Notebook.

ILLUMINATING A ROOM

Suppose we need to decide where to put light fixtures on the ceiling of a room measuring 10 meters by 4 meters by 3 meters high in order to illuminate it best. For aesthetic reasons, we are asked to use a small number of incandescent bulbs. We want the bulbs to total a maximum of 300 watts. For a given number of bulbs, how should they be placed to maximize the intensity of the light in the darkest part of the room? We also would like to see how much improvement there is in going from one 300 watt bulb to two 150 watt bulbs to three 100 watt bulbs, and so on. To keep things simple, we assume that there is no furniture in the room and that the light reflected from the walls is insignificant compared with the direct light from the bulbs.

ONE 300 WATT BULB

If there is only one bulb, then we want to put the bulb in the center of the ceiling. Let's picture how well the floor is illuminated. We introduce coordinates x running from 0 to 10 in the long direction of the room and y running from 0 to 4 in the short direction. The intensity at a given point, measured in watts per square meter, is the power of the bulb, 300, divided by 4π times the square of the distance from the bulb. Since the bulb is 3 meters above the point (5, 2) on the floor, at a point (x, y) on the floor, we can express the intensity as follows:

```
illum[x_, y_] = 300 / (4 Pi ((x - 5)^2 + (y - 2)^2 + 3^2))
```

$$\frac{75}{\pi\,(9 + (-5 + x)^2 + (-2 + y)^2)}$$

We can make a contour plot of this expression over the entire floor. We use the **PlotRange** option to adjust the shading of the plot so that black represents zero intensity and white represents the maximum intensity of $25/(3\pi)$, which occurs directly below the bulb.

```
ContourPlot[illum[x, y], {x, 0, 10}, {y, 0, 4},
  AspectRatio -> Automatic, PlotRange -> {0, 25 / (3 Pi)}];
```

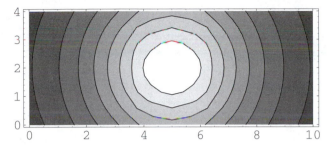

The darkest parts of the floor are the corners. Let us find the intensity of the light at the corners and at the center of the room.

```
illum[0, 0] // N
illum[5, 2] // N
```

0.628243

2.65258

The center of the room, at floor level, is about 4 times as bright as the corners when there is only one bulb on the ceiling. Our objective is to light the room more uniformly using more bulbs with the same total amount of power.

TWO 150 WATT BULBS

In this case we need to decide where to put the two bulbs. Common sense tells us to arrange the bulbs symmetrically along a line down the center of the room in the long direction; that is, along the line $y = 2$. Define a function that gives the intensity of light at a point (x, y) on the floor due to a 150 watt bulb at a position $(d, 2)$ on the ceiling.

```
light[d_, x_, y_] =
  150 / (4 Pi ((x - d) ^2 + (y - 2) ^2 + 3^2))
```

$$\frac{75}{2 \pi \left(9 + (-d + x)^2 + (-2 + y)^2\right)}$$

Let's get an idea of the illumination pattern if we put one light at $d = 3$ and the other at $d = 7$. We use the same values for **PlotRange** so that the shading is comparable to the graph in the previous section but increase the value of **Contours** from its default of 10 so that the number of contours drawn is about the same in the reduced range that the intensities occupy this time.

```
ContourPlot[light[3, x, y] + light[7, x, y],
 {x, 0, 10}, {y, 0, 4}, AspectRatio -> Automatic,
 PlotRange -> {0, 25 / (3 Pi)}, Contours -> 20];
```

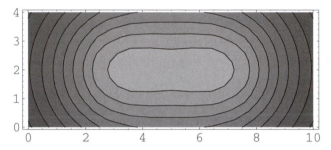

The floor is more evenly lit than with one bulb, but it appears that the bulbs are closer together than they should be. If we move the bulbs farther apart, the center of the room will get dimmer but the corners will get brighter. Let's try changing the location of the lights to $d = 2$ and $d = 8$.

```
ContourPlot[light[2, x, y] + light[8, x, y],
 {x, 0, 10}, {y, 0, 4}, AspectRatio -> Automatic,
 PlotRange -> {0, 25 / (3 Pi)}, Contours -> 30];
```

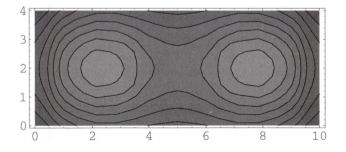

This is an improvement. The corners are still the darkest spots of the room, though the light intensity along the walls toward the middle of the room (near $x = 5$) is diminishing as we move the bulbs farther apart. Still, to illuminate the darkest spots better we should keep moving the bulbs apart. Let's try lights at $d = 1$ and $d = 9$.

```
ContourPlot[light[1, x, y] + light[9, x, y],
  {x, 0, 10}, {y, 0, 4}, AspectRatio -> Automatic,
  PlotRange -> {0, 25/(3 Pi)}, Contours -> 30];
```

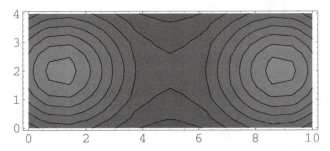

Looking along the long walls, the room is now darker toward the middle than at the corners. This indicates that we have spread the lights too far apart.

We could proceed with further contour plots, but instead let's be systematic about finding the best position for the lights. In general, we can put one light at $x = d$ and the other symmetrically at $x = 10 - d$ for d between 0 and 5. Let's define two functions giving the intensities at, respectively, the corner $(0, 0)$ and the middle $(5, 0)$ of a long wall, due to bulbs at d and $10 - d$.

```
corner[d_] = light[d, 0, 0] + light[10 - d, 0, 0];
middle[d_] = light[d, 5, 0] + light[10 - d, 5, 0];
```

Now we can graph the intensity at $(0, 0)$ as a function of d.

```
graph1 = Plot[corner[d],
   {d, 0, 5}, AxesLabel -> {"d", "intensity"},
   PlotRange -> {0, 1.1}];
```

As expected, the smaller d is, the brighter the corners are. In contrast, the graph for the intensity at (5, 0) should grow as d increases toward 5.

```
graph2 = Plot[middle[d],
   {d, 0, 5}, AxesLabel -> {"d", "intensity"},
   PlotRange -> {0, 1.9}];
```

We are after the value of d for which the lowest of the two numbers on the graphs (corresponding to the darkest point in the room) is as high as possible. We can find this value by showing both curves on one graph.

```
Show[graph1, graph2, PlotRange -> {0, 1.9}];
```

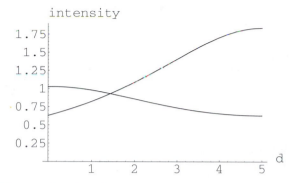

The optimal value of d is at the point of intersection, near 1.4, with minimum intensity a little under 1. To get the optimal value of d, we find exactly where the two curves intersect.

```
Solve[corner[d] == middle[d], d] // N
```

$\{\{d \to 1.44097\}, \{d \to 8.55903\}\}$

So the lights should be placed about 1.44 meters from the short walls. For this configuration, the approximate intensity at the darkest spots on the floor is as follows:

```
{corner[1.44097], middle[1.44097]}
```

$\{0.930127, 0.930125\}$

The darkest spots in the room have intensity around 0.93, as opposed to 0.63 for a single bulb. This represents an improvement of about 50 percent.

THREE 100 WATT BULBS

We redefine the intensity function for 100 watt bulbs.

```
light[d_, x_, y_] =
  100 / (4 Pi ((x - d) ^ 2 + (y - 2) ^ 2 + 3 ^ 2))
```

$$\frac{25}{\pi \left(9 + (-d + x)^2 + (-2 + y)^2\right)}$$

Assume we put one bulb at the center of the room and place the other two symmetrically as before. Here we show the illumination of the floor when the off-center bulbs are 1 meter from the short walls.

```
ContourPlot[
  light[1, x, y] + light[5, x, y] + light[9, x, y],
  {x, 0, 10}, {y, 0, 4}, AspectRatio -> Automatic,
  PlotRange -> {0, 25 / (3 Pi)}, Contours -> 30];
```

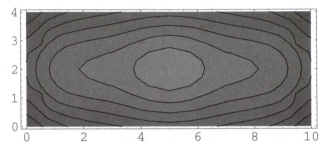

It appears that we should put the bulbs even closer to the walls. (This may not please everyone's aesthetics!) Let d be the distance of the bulbs from the short walls. We define a function giving the intensity at position x along a long wall and then graph the intensity as a function of d for several values of x.

```
intensity[d_, x_] =
  light[d, x, 0] + light[5, x, 0] + light[10 - d, x, 0];
```

```
Plot[Evaluate[Table[intensity[d, x], {x, 0, 5, 0.5}]],
  {d, 0, 5}, AxesLabel -> {"d", "intensity"},
  PlotRange -> {0, 1.9}];
```

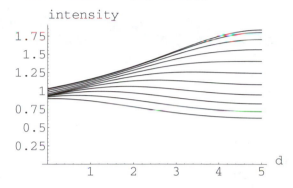

We know that for d near 5, the intensity will be increasing as x increases from 0 to 5, so the bottom curve corresponds to $x = 0$ and the top curve to $x = 5$. Notice that the $x = 0$ curve is the lowest one for all d, and it rises as d decreases. Thus $d = 0$ maximizes the intensity of the darkest spots in the room, which are the corners (corresponding to $x = 0$). There the intensity is as follows:

```
intensity[0, 0] // N
```

0.891971

This is surprising; we do worse than with two bulbs. In going from two bulbs to three, with a decrease in wattage per bulb, we are forced to move wattage away from the ends of the room and bring it back to the center. We could probably improve on the two bulb scenario if we used brighter bulbs at the ends of the room and a dimmer bulb in the center, or if we used four 75 watt bulbs. But our results so far indicate that the amount to be gained in going to more than two bulbs is likely to be small compared with the amount we gained by going from one bulb to two.

MORTGAGE PAYMENTS

We want to understand the relationships among the mortgage payment of a fixed rate mortgage, the principal (the amount borrowed), the annual interest rate, and the period of the loan. We are going to assume that payments are made monthly, even though the interest rate is given as an annual rate. So, one of the things we will need is a way to convert years into months. Let's define

```
months = 1;
years = 12 * months;
peryear = 1 / years;
percent = 1 / 100.0;
```

For example, we can write

```
30 * years
```

```
360
```

to determine the number of monthly payments made on a 30 year loan, and we can write

```
8 * percent * peryear
```

```
0.00666667
```

to convert an annual percentage rate of 8 percent into a monthly rate.

Now let's think about what happens with each monthly payment. Some of the payment is applied to pay the interest for that month, and the remainder is applied to reduce the principal. Let P denote the principal at the beginning of the month, let R denote the amount of the monthly payment, and let J denote the monthly interest rate.

```
interestPaid[P_, J_] := P * J;

reduction[P_, J_, R_] := R - interestPaid[P, J];

newPrincipal[P_, J_, R_] := P - reduction[P, J, R];
```

This allows us to compute a formula for the new principal.

```
newPrincipal[P, J, R]
```

P + J P - R

In order to understand the full relationship among the principal, interest rate, number of payments, and monthly payment, we need to see how the outstanding principal changes over the course of several payments. The simplest way to think about this relationship is to observe that the outstanding principal changes with each payment by the formula we just worked out for computing the new principal after one payment; we simply need to repeat this process. The next series of commands shows how to do this. (The curious double definition of the function `outstanding[N]` is a standard technique in Mathematica to make the function remember values that it has computed earlier. See Section 2.4.9 of *The Mathematica Book* by Steven Wolfram.)

```
outstanding[0] = P;
outstanding[N_] := outstanding[N] =
            newPrincipal[outstanding[N - 1], J, R]
```

For example, here is the amount of the principal still outstanding after each of the first six payments:

```
Table[Simplify[outstanding[n]], {n, 0, 6}] // TableForm
```

P

P + J P - R

$(1 + J)^2 P - (2 + J) R$

$(1 + J)^3 P - (3 + 3 J + J^2) R$

$(1 + J)^4 P - (4 + 6 J + 4 J^2 + J^3) R$

$(1 + J)^5 P - (5 + 10 J + 10 J^2 + 5 J^3 + J^4) R$

$(1 + J)^6 P - (6 + 15 J + 20 J^2 + 15 J^3 + 6 J^4 + J^5) R$

Next, we'll try to find a better formula for the outstanding principal. It's clear from our examples that there will always be a term of the form $(1 + J)^n P$. However, we need a better formula for the term involving R. The coefficients of powers of J in this term are reminiscent of the binomial coefficients. For example, we have

```
Expand[(1 + J)^6]
```

$1 + 6 J + 15 J^2 + 20 J^3 + 15 J^4 + 6 J^5 + J^6$

With a minor adjustment, we can get the exact term.

```
Expand[((1 + J)^6 - 1)/J]
```

$6 + 15 J + 20 J^2 + 15 J^3 + 6 J^4 + J^5$

So, a formula for the outstanding principal is

```
outstandingPrincipal =
   (1 + J)^N * P - (((1 + J)^N - 1)/J) * R
```

$(1 + J)^N P - \dfrac{(-1 + (1 + J)^N) R}{J}$

Now suppose that after N payments the loan is paid off. Then the outstanding principal is zero. By setting **outstandingPrincipal** to zero and solving the resulting equation for R, we can compute the monthly payment as a function of the principal, interest rate, and number of payments.

```
Solve[outstandingPrincipal == 0, R]
```

$\left\{\left\{R \to \dfrac{J\,(1 + J)^N\,P}{-1 + (1 + J)^N}\right\}\right\}$

```
payment[P_, J_, N_] := J * (1 + J)^N * P / ((1 + J)^N - 1)
```

For example, the payment on a loan of $150,000 at 8 percent for 30 years is

```
payment[150000, 8 * percent * peryear, 30 * years]
```

```
1100.65
```

We may also want to determine the amount of money that can be borrowed as a function of the amount we are able to pay each month. We simply solve our equation for P in terms of the remaining variables.

```
Solve[outstandingPrincipal == 0, P]
```

$\left\{\left\{P \to \dfrac{(1 + J)^{-N}\,(-1 + (1 + J)^N)\,R}{J}\right\}\right\}$

```
loanAmount[R_, J_, N_] :=
  ((1 + J)^N - 1) * R / (J * (1 + J)^N)
```

For example, suppose that we can afford to pay $1500 per month, and that the interest rate on a 30 year loan is 8 percent. Then the amount of money that can be borrowed is

```
loanAmount[1500, 8 * percent * peryear, 30 * years]
```

```
204425.
```

As a final piece of the analysis, we are going to write a function that will produce a table of values showing how much of each of a series of payments is allocated toward the interest payment, and how much is used to reduce the principal. The function takes as inputs the initial principal, the annual interest rate, the monthly payment, and the number of payments to be made during the period of time covered by the table. We use the Mathematica commands **Module** and **Do** to write a function that can repeat a process a fixed number of times, using local variables to store the intermediate results of the computation.

```
several[P_, J_, R_, N_] :=
  Module[{p = P, onerow, allrows = {{"principal",
       "interest paid", "principal paid"}}}, Do[
    onerow = {p, interestPaid[p, J], reduction[p, J, R]};
    allrows = Join[allrows, {onerow}];
    p = newPrincipal[p, J, R], {i, 1, N}];
  allrows]
```

Let's see what happens if we make 1 year's worth of $1100.65 payments on a $150,000 loan at an annual interest rate of 8 percent.

```
several[150000,
   8 * percent * peryear, 1100.65, 12 months] //
  TableForm
```

principal	interest paid	principal paid
150000	1000.	100.65
149899.	999.329	101.321
149798.	998.654	101.996
149696.	997.974	102.676
149593.	997.289	103.361
149490.	996.6	104.05
149386.	995.906	104.744
149281.	995.208	105.442
149176.	994.505	106.145
149070.	993.797	106.853
148963.	993.085	107.565
148855.	992.368	108.282

Using similar techniques, we can determine the total amount of interest paid over the life of a loan. In order to do this, we need to know the principal, the interest rate, and the number of payments.

```
totalInterest[P_, J_, N_ ] :=
 Module[{ip = 0, p = P, r = payment[P, J, N]},
   Do[ip += interestPaid[p, J];
    p -= reduction[p, J, r], {i, N}];
   ip]
```

For example, let's continue to look at the case of a 30 year mortgage at 8 percent. With a principal of

```
prin = 150000;
```

we pay a total interest of

```
inter = totalInterest[prin, 8 * percent * peryear, 30 years]
246233.
```

Here is a pie chart showing the relative amounts paid in principal and interest over the life of the loan:

```
<< Graphics`Graphics`
PieChart[{prin, inter},
 PieStyle -> {GrayLevel[0.4], GrayLevel[0.8]},
 PieLabels -> {"Principal", "Interest"}];
```

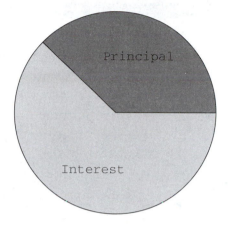

CRYPTOGRAPHY

In this Notebook, we are going to use Mathematica to implement some simple encryption schemes and to analyze and decode messages.

ADDITIVE CIPHERS

One of the simplest codes is an *additive cipher*, obtained by replacing each letter in a message by the letter exactly n places to the right of it in the alphabet, for some fixed number n. When the end of the alphabet is reached, the count continues from the beginning of the alphabet. For example, the additive cipher corresponding to $n = 5$ would replace "A" by "F" and "W" by "C".

To implement this cipher, we can use Mathematica's built-in string manipulation functions. Since a Mathematica string must be surrounded by double quotes, we can define the string consisting of the letters in the alphabet by

```
alphabet = "ABCDEFGHIJKLMNOPQRSTUVWXYZ"
```

ABCDEFGHIJKLMNOPQRSTUVWXYZ

To encrypt a message, we want to apply a list of replacement rules to a message string. Continuing with the example of the additive cipher for $n = 5$, we want to use the replacement rules `"A" -> "F"`, `"B" -> "G"`, and so on. It would be tedious to type all these replacement rules, so we will automate the process instead. To create the replacement rule for a given letter, say, the ninth letter of the alphabet, we type

```
StringTake[alphabet, {9}] ->
  StringTake[alphabet, {Mod[(9 - 1) + 5, 26] + 1}]
```

I → N

The preceding command makes a replacement rule using the 9th letter of the alphabet and the $(9 + 5)$th letter of the alphabet. Since there are only 26 letters in the alphabet, we use the **Mod** command to make sure that numbers larger than 26 wrap around to the beginning of the alphabet.

Now that we have a command that does one letter at a time, we can use the **Table** command to do the whole alphabet at once.

```
encrypt5 = Table[StringTake[alphabet, {i}] ->
    StringTake[alphabet, {Mod[(i - 1) + 5, 26] + 1}],
  {i, 1, 26}]
```

{A → F, B → G, C → H, D → I, E → J, F → K, G → L, H → M, I → N,
J → O, K → P, L → Q, M → R, N → S, O → T, P → U, Q → V,
R → W, S → X, T → Y, U → Z, V → A, W → B, X → C, Y → D, Z → E}

To proceed, we need a message to encrypt. Here's a simple one:

```
cleartext = "This is the message I want to encrypt"
```

This is the message I want to encrypt

In order to use the replacement rules, we must put the message in uppercase.

```
cleartext = ToUpperCase[cleartext]
```

THIS IS THE MESSAGE I WANT TO ENCRYPT

Now we encrypt the message by using **StringReplace** together with the replacement rules in **encrypt5**.

```
ciphertext = StringReplace[cleartext, encrypt5]
```

YMNX NX YMJ RJXXFLJ N BFSY YT JSHWDUY

Finally, we should eliminate the spaces in the message to make it harder to decipher.

```
ciphertext = StringReplace[ciphertext, " " -> ""]
```

YMNXNXYMJRJXXFLJNBFSYYTJSHWDUY

We can decrypt the message by applying the opposite set of replacement rules as follows:

```
decrypt5 = Table[StringTake[alphabet, {i}] ->
    StringTake[alphabet, {Mod[(i - 1) - 5, 26] + 1}],
  {i, 1, 26}]
```

$\{A \to V, B \to W, C \to X, D \to Y, E \to Z, F \to A, G \to B, H \to C, I \to D,$
$J \to E, K \to F, L \to G, M \to H, N \to I, O \to J, P \to K, Q \to L,$
$R \to M, S \to N, T \to O, U \to P, V \to Q, W \to R, X \to S, Y \to T, Z \to U\}$

```
StringReplace[ciphertext, decrypt5]
```

THISISTHEMESSAGEIWANTTOENCRYPT

BREAKING THE CODE

Let's define some functions that will automate the process of encryption and decryption.

```
encrypt[n_] :=
 Table[StringTake[alphabet, {i}] -> StringTake[
    alphabet, {Mod[(i - 1) + n, 26] + 1}], {i, 1, 26}]
decrypt[n_] := Table[StringTake[alphabet, {i}] ->
   StringTake[alphabet, {Mod[(i - 1) - n, 26] + 1}],
  {i, 1, 26}]

additiveEncode[cleartext_, key_] :=
 StringReplace[cleartext, encrypt[key]]
additiveDecode[ciphertext_, key_] :=
 StringReplace[ciphertext, decrypt[key]]
```

Here is a quote that has been encoded using an additive cipher.

```
cipherquote =
 "ABJRAGREGNVAPBAWRPGHERBSNGVZRJURAPERRCVATZHEZHENAQGURC.
   BEVATQNEXSVYYFGURJVQRIRFFRYBSGURHAVIREFRSEBZPNZCGBPN.
   ZCGUEBHTUGURSBHYJBZOBSAVTUGGURUHZBSRVGURENEZLFGVYYLF.
   BHAQFGUNGGURSVKRQFRAGVARYFNYZBFGERPRVIRGURFRPERGJUVF.
   CREFBSRNPUBGUREFJNGPUSVERNAFJREFSVERNAQGUEBHTUGURVEC.
   NYLSYNZRFRNPUONGGYRFRRFGURBGUREFHZOREQSNPRFGRRQGUERN.
   GRAFFGRRQVAUVTUNAQOBNFGSHYARVTUFCVREPVATGURAVTUGFQHY.
   YRNENAQSEBZGURGRAGFGURNEZBHEREFNPPBZCYVFUVATGURXAVTU.
   GFJVGUOHFLUNZZREFPYBFVATEVIRGFHCTVIRQERNQSHYABGRBSCE.
   RCNENGVBA";
```

How can we decode it? One approach would be to use brute force. Since there are only 26 different additive ciphers, we could simply apply our user-defined function **additiveDecode** to the message using each of the numbers 1 through 26 as keys and look for an output that makes sense. Here is a more sophisticated approach. It is known that the letter "E" occurs more often than any other letter in the English language. One estimate is that the letter "E" comprises 12.7 percent of the letters in a typical English text. The next most frequent letter is "T", at 9.1 percent. If we can figure out which letter in the ciphertext corresponds to the letter "E", then we can decipher the message. Let's analyze the message to see which letter occurs most often.

To do this, we first convert the message to a list (as opposed to a string) and then count the occurrences of each letter.

```
cipherlist = Characters[cipherquote];
countoccurrences[x_] := {Count[cipherlist, x], x}

Map[countoccurrences, Characters[alphabet]]
```

{{28, A}, {26, B}, {11, C}, {0, D}, {35, E}, {34, F},
 {46, G}, {16, H}, {5, I}, {8, J}, {1, K}, {4, L}, {0, M},
 {29, N}, {5, O}, {15, P}, {14, Q}, {67, R}, {17, S},
 {13, T}, {37, U}, {31, V}, {1, W}, {2, X}, {17, Y}, {17, Z}}

The most frequent letter in the ciphertext is "R", so we can be reasonably sure that "E" has been encoded as "R". Thus the shift in the additive cipher is 13, the distance between "E" and "R" in the alphabet. You can apply the function **additiveDecode[cipherquote, 13]** to see the decoded message.

An additive cipher is so easy to break that no self-respecting cryptanalyst would use it. In 1586, the French diplomat Blaise de Vigenere introduced a more complicated cipher. His idea was to use one additive cipher to encode the first letter of a message, a different additive cipher to encode the second letter, and so on. The main problem is to keep track of which additive cipher to use for each letter. In Vigenere ciphers, this is done by repeatedly writing a keyword above the message, where each letter of the keyword determines the additive cipher to use for the corresponding letter of the message. In spite of the complications introduced by the keyword, a Vigenere cipher can also be attacked by statistical methods, which start by attempting to estimate the length of the keyword.

PUBLIC KEY CRYPTOGRAPHY

Modern methods in cryptography evade elementary statistical analysis by encoding blocks of letters as numbers. They also rely on powerful techniques from the theory of prime numbers and factorization. As our final example, we will discuss the RSA (Rivest-Shamir-Adleman) encryption scheme. This method has another interesting aspect: you can transmit part of the key publicly, since the key used to encrypt messages is different from the key used to decrypt them.

This encryption system requires us to choose two large prime numbers. For practical use, the primes should have at least 100 decimal digits; finding such primes is an adventure of its own. For our example, however, we'll let Mathematica generate some smaller prime numbers.

```
? Prime
```

```
Prime[n] gives the nth prime number.
```

```
p = Prime[1000076543]
```

```
22803593311
```

```
q = Prime[98123654]
```

```
1997881807
```

For the method to work, the individual prime numbers need to be kept secret. The product, however, is part of the public key.

```
pq = p * q
```

```
45558884210273792977
```

Notice that the product has approximately twice as many digits as the individual factors. In order to break the code, someone would have to factor this product. The strength of the code relies on the fact that it is still extremely difficult (even with powerful computers) to factor integers with more than 200 digits. Consequently, it is also difficult to compute a number theoretic function called the Euler ϕ function; to compute it, you need to know the factorization. In our case, we started by choosing p and q ourselves, so we know the value $\phi(p\,q)$. Here it is:

```
phi = (p - 1) * (q - 1)
```

```
45558884185472317860
```

The Euler ϕ function is built into Mathematica.

```
EulerPhi[pq]
```

45558884185472317860

The fact that Mathematica can factor $p\,q$ to compute this value tells us that our example is not secure.

Now we are ready to pick the remainder of the public key. We can choose almost any random integer less than ϕ. (The number we choose cannot share a common factor with ϕ.)

```
e = Random[Integer, phi - 1];
While[GCD[e, phi] != 1, e = Random[Integer, phi - 1];]
e
```

38359051528648284757

Now we can compute the secret part of the key, which will be used to decrypt messages.

```
d = PowerMod[e, -1, phi]
```

22525260912785774053

The magic that makes everything work is a theorem of Leonhard Euler. This theorem tells us that any number A, when raised to the $e * d$ power, leaves a remainder equal to A upon division by $p\,q$. Here are some examples to verify that statement:

```
testEuler[A_] := PowerMod[A, e * d, pq]

testEuler[121]
```

121

```
testEuler[3456789]
```

3456789

Here are the functions that encode and decode messages:

```
rsaEncode[A_] := PowerMod[A, e, pq]
rsaDecode[A_] := PowerMod[A, d, pq]
```

Now let's take a message (in the form of an integer) and encrypt it.

```
hidden = rsaEncode[123123123123]
```

1507007402154706745

As you can see, the encrypted message gives little clue of the repeating pattern in the original integer. However, it can easily be decrypted.

```
rsaDecode[hidden]
```

123123123123

One step remains before we can use this method to encrypt a message written in standard English. We have to convert the letters into integers that can be encrypted by this method. But that's quite easy on a computer; all those letters are stored as numbers anyway.

For an excellent introduction to cryptography, see A. Beutelspacher, *Cryptography*, Mathematical Association of America, 1994.

FIBONACCI NUMBERS

We are going to study a sequence of numbers known as the Fibonacci numbers. These numbers arise in many situations, one of which we now describe.

Suppose on a certain day we have 1 pair of baby rabbits, and we know that in 1 month they will have matured to adulthood, and then 1 month later will produce a pair of baby rabbits, then another pair of babies 2 months later, another pair 3 months later, and so on. Furthermore, each new pair of baby rabbits will reach adulthood in 1 month and then produce a pair of babies 1 month later and each month thereafter. How many adult pairs will there be after 5 months, after 30 months, after any specific number of months? The numbers that answer these questions are called the *Fibonacci numbers*. If we denote the number of adult pairs after n months by F_n, then we want to find or calculate F_n. The first few Fibonacci numbers are easy to calculate by following the generations of our rabbit colony month by month; we find that $F_0 = 0$, $F_1 = 1$, $F_2 = 1$, $F_3 = 2$, and $F_4 = 3$. We would like to have a simple systematic way to find F_n for any n; we will discuss several ways to calculate F_n.

THE BUILT-IN FUNCTION FIBONACCI

Let's see if Mathematica has a built-in function for computing Fibonacci numbers.

```
? Fib*
```

```
Fibonacci[n] gives the nth Fibonacci number. Fibonacci[
   n, x] gives the nth Fibonacci polynomial, using
   x as the variable.
```

So we see that **Fibonacci[n]** gives F_n. We illustrate the use of this command.

```
Fibonacci[0]
Fibonacci[1]
Fibonacci[2]
Fibonacci[3]
```

```
0

1

1

2
```

These results confirm the values previously calculated. And the following results answer the specific questions asked previously.

```
Fibonacci[5]
Fibonacci[30]
```

```
5

832040
```

So there are 5 pairs of adult rabbits after 5 months, and 832,040 adult pairs after 30 months. We can also make a table of Fibonacci numbers with the commands **Table** and **TableForm.** Here is a table of the first 16 Fibonacci numbers:

```
fibtable = Table[{n, Fibonacci[n]}, {n, 0, 15}]
{{0, 0}, {1, 1}, {2, 1}, {3, 2}, {4, 3}, {5, 5},
 {6, 8}, {7, 13}, {8, 21}, {9, 34}, {10, 55}, {11, 89},
 {12, 144}, {13, 233}, {14, 377}, {15, 610}}
```

```
TableForm[fibtable, TableDirections -> {Row, Column},
 TableHeadings -> {None, {"n", "F[n]"}},
 TableSpacing -> {1, 1}]
```

n	0	1	2	3	4	5	6	7	8	9	10	11	12	13	14	15
F[n]	0	1	1	2	3	5	8	13	21	34	55	89	144	233	377	610

THE FUNDAMENTAL RECURRENCE RELATION

We have used the **Fibonacci** command as a "black box" with no idea how the calculations are done. We now turn to a discussion of the computation of Fibonacci numbers. In addition to explaining methods of computation, this discussion will introduce several useful Mathematica commands. In this section we show that the F_n's satisfy a recurrence relation. From the earlier month-by-month calculation we see that the number of adult pairs after n months equals the number of adult pairs after $n-1$ months plus the number of baby pairs after $n-1$ months. Thus, since the number of baby pairs after $n-1$ months equals the number of adult pairs after $n-2$ months, we see that the number of adult pairs after n months equals the number of adult pairs after $n-1$ months plus the number of adult pairs after $n-2$ months.

If we let F_n denote the number of adult pairs after n months, we can state this principle as

(1a) $F_n = F_{n-1} + F_{n-2}$, for all $n \geq 2$.

This formula, which is called a recurrence relation, together with the values

(1b) $F_0 = 0, F_1 = 1,$

which are called initial values for the sequence F_n, provides a procedure for calculating F_n for any n: $F_4 = 3$, $F_5 = 5$, and so on. We can thus calculate any Fibonacci number, and hence the number of adult pairs of rabbits after any number of months.

It would be useful, however, to have a formula for F_n that depends only on n, and not on the two previous Fibonacci numbers. Such a formula can be obtained by solving the recurrence relation (1a) with initial values (1b). This can be done with the **RSolve** command, which is part of the **DiscreteMath** package. We first load the command and then use it to solve (1a,b).

```
<< DiscreteMath`RSolve`
```

```
sol = RSolve[
   {F[n] == F[n - 1] + F[n - 2], F[0] == 0, F[1] == 1},
   F[n], n]
```

$$\left\{ \left\{ F[n] \to -\frac{\left(\frac{1}{2} - \frac{\sqrt{5}}{2}\right)^n - \left(\frac{1}{2}\left(1 + \sqrt{5}\right)\right)^n}{\sqrt{5}} \right\} \right\}$$

```
fibtemp[n_] = F[n] /. First[sol]
```

$$-\frac{\left(\frac{1}{2} - \frac{\sqrt{5}}{2}\right)^n - \left(\frac{1}{2}\left(1 + \sqrt{5}\right)\right)^n}{\sqrt{5}}$$

```
fibtemp[2]
```

$$-\frac{\left(\frac{1}{2} - \frac{\sqrt{5}}{2}\right)^2 - \frac{1}{4}\left(1 + \sqrt{5}\right)^2}{\sqrt{5}}$$

Though **fibtemp[n]** is the correct formula, it does not present its value in simplified form. We thus modify **fibtemp** by incorporating the **Simplify** command using delayed evaluation:

```
fib[n_] := Simplify[fibtemp[n]]
```

We illustrate the use of **fib** by computing a few values.

```
fib[0]
fib[3]
fib[5]

0

2

5
```

We see that `fib` produces the same values as the `Fibonacci` command.

CALCULATION VIA POWERS OF A MATRIX

The recurrence relation (1a,b) can be conveniently expressed in vector-matrix form. Introduce the matrix $A = \begin{pmatrix} 1 & 1 \\ 1 & 0 \end{pmatrix}$ and the vector $\boldsymbol{u}_n = \begin{pmatrix} F_{n+1} \\ F_n \end{pmatrix}$, and consider the vector-matrix recurrence relation

(2a) $\begin{pmatrix} F_{n+1} \\ F_n \end{pmatrix} = \boldsymbol{u}_n = A\,\boldsymbol{u}_{n-1} = \begin{pmatrix} 1 & 1 \\ 1 & 0 \end{pmatrix}\begin{pmatrix} F_n \\ F_{n-1} \end{pmatrix}$, for all $n \geq 1$.

Carrying out the matrix multiplication, we see that (2a) reduces to the two equations $F_{n+1} = F_n + F_{n-1}$ and $F_n = F_n$. The first of these equations is the recurrence relation (1a) and the second is automatically true. So (2a) is just a restatement of (1a). The vector form of the initial values (1b) is

(2b) $\boldsymbol{u}_0 = \begin{pmatrix} F_1 \\ F_0 \end{pmatrix} = \begin{pmatrix} 1 \\ 0 \end{pmatrix}$.

Using (2a) repeatedly, together with (2b), we see that $\boldsymbol{u}_1 = A\,\boldsymbol{u}_0$, $\boldsymbol{u}_2 = A\,\boldsymbol{u}_1 = A(A\,\boldsymbol{u}_0) = A^2\,\boldsymbol{u}_0$, and in general

(3) $\boldsymbol{u}_n = A^n\,\boldsymbol{u}_0$, for all $n \geq 1$.

That is, $\boldsymbol{u}_n = A^n\,\boldsymbol{u}_0$ is the solution of the vector-matrix recurrence relation (2a,b). So, we can calculate F_n by using (3) to calculate $\boldsymbol{u}_n$, and then finding F_n in the second component of $\boldsymbol{u}_n$. Our problem has been reduced to calculating powers of A, and multiplying $\boldsymbol{u}_0$ by them. Let's carry out this procedure.

```
A = {{1, 1}, {1, 0}}
```

```
{{1, 1}, {1, 0}}
```

To write A in usual matrix notation, use the **MatrixForm** command.

```
MatrixForm[A]
```

$$\begin{pmatrix} 1 & 1 \\ 1 & 0 \end{pmatrix}$$

```
u0 = {1, 0}
```

```
{1, 0}
```

Powers of a matrix are calculated with the **MatrixPower** command, and not with **A^n**. We check the online help for **MatrixPower,** redefine **fib** using powers of A, and then compute a few Fibonacci numbers.

```
? MatrixPower
```

```
MatrixPower[mat, n] gives the nth matrix power of mat.
```

```
Clear[fib]
fib[n_] := Last[MatrixPower[A, n] . u0]
```

The use of **Last** extracts the second component of the vector $A^n \boldsymbol{u}_0$. Note that matrix-vector multiplication is indicated by **.** rather than by *.

```
fib[1]
fib[5]
fib[30]
```

```
1
```

```
5
```

```
832040
```

USING EIGENPAIRS TO CALCULATE A^n

Powers of a matrix can be readily calculated if we know the eigenpairs of the matrix. Recall that a pair $(\lambda, \boldsymbol{x})$ consisting of a number λ and a vector $\boldsymbol{x}$ is an eigenpair of A if $A\boldsymbol{x} = \lambda\boldsymbol{x}$ and $\boldsymbol{x} \neq 0$. The number λ is called an eigenvalue of A and the vector $\boldsymbol{x}$ is called a corresponding eigenvector. The eigenpairs of A are found with the **Eigensystem** command.

```
vals = Eigensystem[A]
```

$$\left\{\left\{\frac{1}{2}\left(1 - \sqrt{5}\right), \frac{1}{2}\left(1 + \sqrt{5}\right)\right\}, \left\{\left\{\frac{1}{2}\left(1 - \sqrt{5}\right), 1\right\}, \left\{\frac{1}{2}\left(1 + \sqrt{5}\right), 1\right\}\right\}\right\}$$

The output is a nested list containing first a list of the eigenvalues, then a list of the corresponding eigenvectors. The eigenvalues are

```
λ = First[First[vals]]
```

$$\frac{1}{2}\left(1 - \sqrt{5}\right)$$

and

```
μ = Last[First[vals]]
```

$$\frac{1}{2}\left(1 + \sqrt{5}\right)$$

The corresponding eigenvectors are

```
x = First[Last[vals]]
```

$$\left\{\frac{1}{2}\left(1 - \sqrt{5}\right), 1\right\}$$

and

```
y = Last[Last[vals]]
```

$$\left\{\frac{1}{2}\left(1 + \sqrt{5}\right), 1\right\}$$

The importance of eigenvectors in our situation is that powers of A act on them in a very simple manner. From the definition of eigenpairs we know that $A\boldsymbol{x} = \lambda\boldsymbol{x}$, and from this we learn that $A^2\boldsymbol{x} = A(\lambda\boldsymbol{x}) = \lambda(A\boldsymbol{x}) = \lambda^2\boldsymbol{x}$. In general, we have $A^n\boldsymbol{x} = \lambda^n\boldsymbol{x}$. Likewise we have $A^n\boldsymbol{y} = \mu^n\boldsymbol{y}$. So a power of A acts on an eigenvector by multiplying the eigenvector by the corresponding eigenvalue raised to the power. But we are interested in $A^n \, u_0 = A^n \begin{pmatrix} 1 \\ 0 \end{pmatrix}$. This can also be calculated, by first expressing the vector u_0 as a linear combination of x and y (the eigenvectors are a basis for two-dimensional vectors) and then applying A^n to this linear combination. To express u_0 as a linear combination of x and y we find coefficients a and b so that

$$u_0 = a \, x + b \, y.$$

It is easily seen that $c = \begin{pmatrix} a \\ b \end{pmatrix}$ is the solution of the linear system $M \, c = u_0$, where

```
M = {{λ, μ}, {1, 1}}
```

$$\left\{\left\{ \tfrac{1}{2} \left(1 - \sqrt{5}\right), \ \tfrac{1}{2} \left(1 + \sqrt{5}\right)\right\}, \ \{1, 1\}\right\}$$

So

```
c = LinearSolve[M, u0]
```

$$\left\{-\frac{1}{\sqrt{5}}, \ \frac{1}{\sqrt{5}}\right\}$$

As a check, let's multiply M by c.

```
M.c
```

$$\left\{-\frac{1 - \sqrt{5}}{2\sqrt{5}} + \frac{1 + \sqrt{5}}{2\sqrt{5}}, \ 0\right\}$$

```
Simplify[%]
```

```
{1, 0}
```

So $u_0 = \begin{pmatrix} 1 \\ 0 \end{pmatrix} = \left(-1 / \sqrt{5}\right) x + \left(1 / \sqrt{5}\right) y$, and thus

$$u_n = A^n \, u_0 = \left(-1 / \sqrt{5}\right) \lambda^n \, x + \left(1 / \sqrt{5}\right) \mu^n \, y.$$

We have reduced the calculation of $A^n u_0$ to the calculation of λ^n and μ^n. Since F_n is the second component of u_n we see that

(4) $F_n = \left(-1/\sqrt{5}\right)\lambda^n + \left(1/\sqrt{5}\right)\mu^n$

$$= \left(-1/\sqrt{5}\right)\left((1-\sqrt{5})/2\right)^n + \left(1/\sqrt{5}\right)\left((1+\sqrt{5})/2\right)^n.$$

We have thus derived the formula produced by **RSolve**.

We have one further formula for F_n.

```
N[λ]
N[μ]
```

```
-0.618034
```

```
1.61803
```

Since $|\lambda| < 1$, we see that λ^n is small for n large, and hence that the first term in formula (4) is small. Thus F_n is approximately equal to the second term in (4). But, since F_n is an integer, it must be the nearest integer to the second term. Let's compute these terms for $n = 3$.

```
N[(-1/Sqrt[5]) λ^3]
N[(1/Sqrt[5]) μ^3]
```

```
0.105573
```

```
1.89443
```

We see that F_3 is 2, the closest integer to the second term in (4). The closest integer can be obtained with the **Round** command.

```
Clear[fib]
fib[n_] := Round[(1/Sqrt[5]) ((1 + Sqrt[5]) / 2) ^n]
```

We illustrate the use of this formula by computing a couple of Fibonacci numbers.

```
fib[30]
fib[100]
```

```
832040
```

```
354224848179261915075
```

For further information on Fibonacci numbers, see V. E. Hoggatt, Jr., *Fibonacci and Lucas Numbers*, Houghton Mifflin Company, 1969.

MONTE CARLO SIMULATION

In order to make statistical predictions about the long-term results of a random process, it is often useful to do a simulation based on one's understanding of the underlying probabilities. This procedure is referred to as the *Monte Carlo* method.

As an example, consider a casino game in which a player bets against the house and the house wins 51 percent of the time. The question is, how many games have to be played before the house is reasonably sure of coming out ahead. This scenario is common enough that mathematicians long ago figured out very precisely what the statistics are, but here we want to illustrate how to get a good idea of what can happen in practice without having to absorb a lot of mathematics.

First we define an expression that computes the net revenue to the house for a single game, based on a random number chosen from 1 to 100. If the number chosen is 1 to 51, the house wins one betting unit, whereas if the number exceeds 51, the house loses one unit. In a high-stakes game, each bet may be worth $1000 or more. Thus it is important for the casino to know how bad a losing streak it may have to weather in order to turn a profit ± so that it doesn't go bankrupt first!

```
revenue := If[Random[Integer, {1, 100}] <= 51, 1, -1]
```

We can play the game by evaluating the expression **revenue**. The following command plays the game 10 times and lists the results; *i* is a dummy variable that runs from 1 to 10.

```
Table[revenue, {i, 10}]

{-1, 1, -1, -1, -1, 1, -1, 1, 1, -1}
```

The net profit to the casino after 10 games is found by adding the 10 numbers on the output line. Next we create a function that gives the net profit for the house after n games are played.

```
profit[n_] := Sum[revenue, {i, n}]
```

On average, every 100 games the house should win 51 times and the player(s) should win 49 times, so the net profit to the house should be 2 betting units. Let's see what happens in a few trial runs.

```
Table[profit[100], {i, 10}]
```

$$\{10, 6, -6, 14, -12, 0, -2, 8, 4, 4\}$$

We see that the net profit can fluctuate significantly from one set of 100 games to the next, and there is a sizable probability that the house has lost money after 100 games. To get an idea of how the net profit is likely to be distributed in general, we can repeat the experiment a large number of times and make a histogram of the results.

```
<< Statistics`
<< Graphics`Graphics`
```

Having loaded the Statistics and Graphics add-on packages, we write a function that plays the game n times, records the net profit, and repeats the experiment k times. It then tabulates the results, setting up intervals, or "bins", of length *xstep* centered at *x0*, *x0* + *xstep*, $x0 + 2\,xstep$, $^{\circ}$, *x1;* counting how many times the net profit after n games falls into each interval; and graphing the result as a histogram, or bar chart. The idea is to figure out, in a systematic way, what possible outcomes the casino can reasonably expect after n games.

```
hist[n_, k_, x0_, x1_, xstep_] := GeneralizedBarChart[
  Transpose[{Table[x, {x, x0, x1, xstep}],
    BinCounts[Table[profit[n], {i, k}],
      {x0 - xstep / 2, x1 + xstep / 2, xstep}],
    Table[xstep, {x, x0, x1, xstep}]}],
  PlotRange -> All, AxesOrigin -> {x0 - xstep / 2, 0}]
```

Now we run the function **hist** using $n = 100$ and $k = 100$. Theoretically the house could win or lose up to 100 chips, but in practice we find that nearly all of the outcomes are within 30 (on either side) of the expected value of 2. We choose the upper and lower limits of our histogram accordingly. The vertical axis represents the number of times a given value of the net profit is obtained during the 100 trials. (Since we add up 100 odd numbers to get the net profit, its value must be even.)

```
hist[100, 100, -28, 32, 2];
```

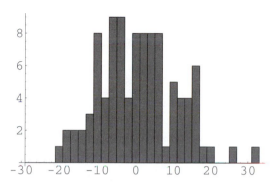

The histogram confirms our impression that there is a wide variation in the outcomes after 100 games. It appears that the casino is about as likely to have lost money as to have profited. However, the distribution shown is irregular enough to indicate that we really should run more trials to see a better approximation to the actual distribution. Let's try 1000 trials.

```
hist[100, 1000, -28, 32, 2];
```

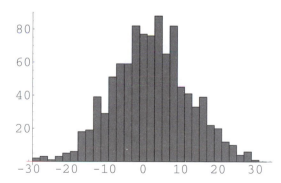

According to the *Central Limit Theorem*, when both *n* and *k* are large, the histogram should be shaped like a "bell curve", and we begin to see this shape emerging. Though it will take a while to run, let's move on to 10,000 trials.

`hist[100, 10000, -28, 32, 2];`

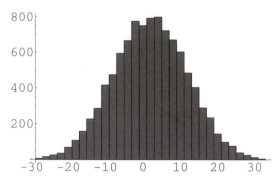

Here we see very clearly the shape of a bell curve. Though we haven't gained much in terms of knowing how likely the house is to be behind after 100 games, and how large its net loss is likely to be in that case, we do gain confidence that our results after 1000 trials are a good depiction of the distribution of possible outcomes.

Now we consider the net profit after 1000 games. We expect on average the house to win 510 games and the player(s) to win 490, for a net profit of 20 chips. Again we start with just 100 trials. Since both the range of possible outcomes and the expected outcome have increased by a factor of 10, we may be inclined to increase the horizontal range of the histogram by a factor of 10 as well.

`hist[1000, 100, -280, 320, 20];`

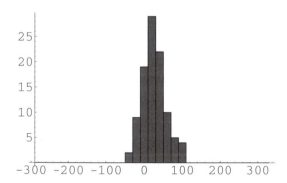

We find that, relatively speaking, the outcomes are clustered much closer together. This reflects the theoretical principle (also a consequence of the *Central Limit Theorem*) that the average "spread" of outcomes after a large number of trials should be proportional to the square root of n, the number of games played in each trial. This is important for the casino, since if the spread were proportional to n, then the casino could never be very sure of making a profit. When we increase n by a factor of 10, the spread should only increase by a factor of $\sqrt{10}$, or a little more than 3. Let's adjust the range of our histograms accordingly.

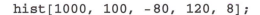

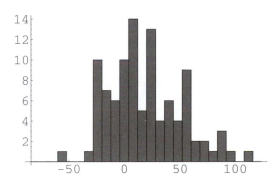

We see that after 1000 games, the house is definitely more likely to be ahead than behind. However, the chances of being behind are still sizable. Let's repeat with 1000 trials to be more sure of our results.

`hist[1000, 1000, -80, 120, 8];`

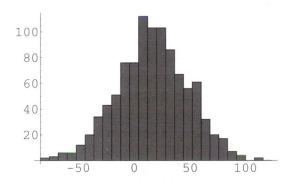

We see the bell curve shape emerging again. Though it is unlikely, the chance that the house is behind by more than 50 chips after 1000 games is not insignificant. If each chip is worth $1000, then we might advise the casino to have at least $100,000 cash on hand to be prepared for this possibility. Maybe even that is not enough ± to see we would have to experiment further.

Finally, let's see what happens after 10,000 games. We expect on average the house to be ahead by 200 chips at this point, and, on the basis of our earlier discussion, the range of values we use to make the histogram need only go up by a factor of 3 or so from the previous case. Even 100 trials will take a while to run now, but we have to start somewhere.

```
hist[10000, 100, -100, 500, 20];
```

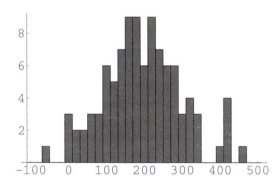

It seems that turning a profit after 10,000 games is highly likely, but with only 100 trials we do not get such a good idea of the worst-case scenario. Though it will take a good bit of time, we should certainly do 1000 trials or more if we are considering putting our money into such a venture. If you run the following command, you may want to take a long break from the computer and come back later to see what happened.

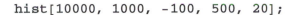

```
hist[10000, 1000, -100, 500, 20];
```

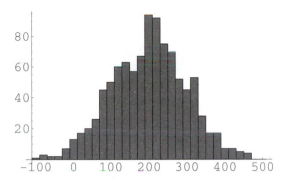

The chances of a loss after 10,000 games look quite small; nevertheless, the possibility cannot be ignored, and we might judge that the house should not rule out being behind at some point by 100 or more chips. However, the overall upward trend seems clear, and we may expect that after 100,000 games the casino is overwhelmingly likely to have made a profit. On the basis of our previous observations of the growth of the spread of outcomes, we expect that most of the time the net profit will be within 1000 of the expected value of 2000. We now show the results of 10 trials of 100,000 games:

```
Table[profit[100000], {i, 10}]
```

{2286, 2508, 2624, 2118, 2406, 2262, 1902, 1772, 1276, 1844}

POPULATION DYNAMICS

We are going to look at two models for population growth of a species. The first is a standard exponential growth/decay model that describes quite well the population of a species becoming extinct, or the short-term behavior of a population growing in an unchecked fashion. The second, more realistic model describes the growth of a species subject to constraints of space, food supply, and competitors/predators.

EXPONENTIAL GROWTH/DECAY

We assume that the species starts with an initial population P_0. The population after n time units is denoted P_n. Suppose that in each time interval, the population increases or decreases by a fixed proportion of its value at the beginning of the interval. Thus $P_n = P_{n-1} + r\,P_{n-1}$, $n \geq 1$. The constant r represents the difference between the birth rate and the death rate. The population increases if r is positive, decreases if r is negative, and remains fixed if $r = 0$. We can express this in Mathematica via

```
P[n_] := (1 + r) P[n - 1]
```

Let's compute two populations at five year intervals for different values of r:

```
r = 0.1; P[0] = 100; Table[P[n], {n, 0, 100, 5}]
```

```
{100, 161.051, 259.374, 417.725, 672.75, 1083.47,
  1744.94, 2810.24, 4525.93, 7289.05, 11739.1, 18905.9,
  30448.2, 49037.1, 78974.7, 127190., 204840., 329897.,
  531302., 855668., 1.37806 × 10^6}
```

```
r = -0.1; P[0] = 100; Table[P[n], {n, 0, 100, 5}]
```

```
{100, 59.049, 34.8678, 20.5891, 12.1577, 7.17898,
  4.23912, 2.50316, 1.47809, 0.872796, 0.515378,
  0.304325, 0.179701, 0.106112, 0.0626579, 0.0369988,
  0.0218475, 0.0129007, 0.00761773, 0.0044982, 0.00265614}
```

In the first case, the population is growing rapidly; in the second, decaying rapidly. In fact, it is clear from the model that, for any n, the quotient $P_n / P_{n-1} = (1 + r)$, and therefore it follows that $P_n = P_0(1 + r)^n$, $n \geq 0$. This accounts for the expression *exponential growth/decay*. The model predicts a population growth without bound (for growing populations) and is therefore not realistic. Our next model allows for a check on the population caused by limited space, limited food supply, competitors, and predators.

LOGISTIC GROWTH

The previous model assumes that the relative change in population is constant, that is

$$\frac{P_{n+1} - P_n}{P_n} = r.$$

Now let's build in a term that holds down the growth, namely

$$\frac{P_{n+1} - P_n}{P_n} = r - u\, P_n.$$

We shall simplify matters by assuming that $u = 1 + r$, so that our recursion relation becomes

$$P_{n+1} = u\, P_n (1 - P_n),$$

where u is a positive constant. In this model, the population P is constrained to lie between 0 and 1 and should be interpreted as a percentage of a maximum possible population in the environment in question.

This time we will use the Mathematica commands **Nest** and **NestList** to automate the computations. Here are explanations of the commands:

```
? Nest
```

```
Nest[f, expr, n] gives an expression with f applied
   n times to expr.
```

```
? NestList
```

```
NestList[f, expr, n] gives a list of the results
   of applying f to expr 0 through n times.
```

Thus **Nest[f, 1, 10]** computes $f(f(^\circ \ (f(1))^\circ \ )$ with 10 evaluations of the function, and **NestList[f, 1, 10]** lists all the intervening iterates. Now let's compute a few examples.

```
Clear[q]
```

```
q[u_][x_] := u * x * (1 - x)
```

```
Nest[q[0.5], 0.5, 20]
```

1.87353×10^{-7}

```
NestList[q[1], 0.5, 20]
```

{0.5, 0.25, 0.1875, 0.152344, 0.129135, 0.112459,
 0.0998122, 0.0898497, 0.0817767, 0.0750893, 0.0694509,
 0.0646275, 0.0604508, 0.0567965, 0.0535706, 0.0507008,
 0.0481302, 0.0458137, 0.0437148, 0.0418038, 0.0400563}

```
NestList[q[1.5], 0.5, 20]
```

{0.5, 0.375, 0.351563, 0.341949, 0.33753, 0.335405,
 0.334363, 0.333847, 0.33359, 0.333461, 0.333397,
 0.333365, 0.333349, 0.333341, 0.333337, 0.333335,
 0.333334, 0.333334, 0.333334, 0.333333, 0.333333}

```
NestList[q[3.4], 0.5, 20]
```

{0.5, 0.85, 0.4335, 0.834964, 0.468516, 0.84663,
 0.441482, 0.838357, 0.460749, 0.844762, 0.445874,
 0.840039, 0.456869, 0.843675, 0.448417, 0.840953,
 0.454753, 0.843039, 0.449902, 0.841467, 0.453562}

In the first computation, we have used the **Nest** command to compute the population density after 20 time intervals, assuming a logistic growth constant $u = 0.5$ and an initial population density of 50 percent. The population seems to be dying out. In the remaining examples, we kept the initial population density at 50 percent, and we used **NestList** to generate a list of densities for the first 20 time intervals. The only thing we varied was the logistic growth constant. In the second example, with a growth constant $u = 1$, once again the population is dying out. In the third example, with a growth constant of 1.5, the population seems to be stabilizing at 33.3° percent. Finally, in the last example, with a constant of 3.4 the population seems to oscillate between densities of approximately 45 percent and 84 percent.

These examples illustrate the remarkable features of the logistic population dynamics model. This model has been studied for more than 150 years, its origins lying in an analysis by the Belgian mathematician

Verhulst. Here are some of the facts associated with this model. We will corroborate some of them with Mathematica. In particular, we shall use **ListPlot** and **BarChart** to display some of the data.

(1) The logistic constant cannot be larger than 4.

In order for the model to work, the output at any point must be between 0 and 1. But the parabola $u\,x(1-x)$, for $0 \le x \le 1$, has its maximum height when $x = 1/2$, where its value is $u/4$. To keep that number between 0 and 1, we must restrict $u \le 4$. Here is what happens if u is bigger than 4:

```
Nest[q[4.5], 0.9, 10]
```
-3.49103×10^{72}

(2) If $0 \le u \le 1$, the population density tends to zero for any initial configuration.

```
Nest[q[0.8], 0.99, 100]
```
1.93952×10^{-12}

```
lis1 = NestList[q[1], 0.75, 20]
```
{0.75, 0.1875, 0.152344, 0.129135, 0.112459, 0.0998122,
 0.0898497, 0.0817767, 0.0750893, 0.0694509, 0.0646275,
 0.0604508, 0.0567965, 0.0535706, 0.0507008, 0.0481302,
 0.0458137, 0.0437148, 0.0418038, 0.0400563, 0.0384518}

Now let's use **ListPlot** and **BarChart** to display this data.

```
ListPlot[lis1, PlotJoined -> True];
```

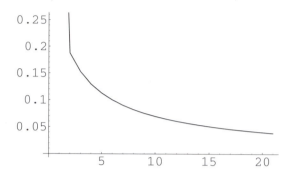

```
<< Graphics`Graphics`
BarChart[lis1, Ticks -> {None, Automatic}];
```

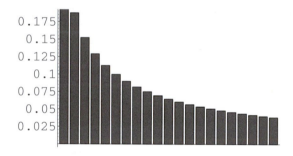

(3) If $1 < u \leq 3$, the population will stabilize at density $1 - 1/u$ for any initial density other than zero.

The third of the original four examples corroborates the assertion (with $u = 1.5$ and $1 - 1/u = 1/3$). In the following examples, we set $u = 2, 2.5$, and 3, respectively, so that $1 - 1/u$ equals 0.5, 0.6, and 0.666° , respectively. The convergence in the last computation is rather slow (as one might expect from a boundary case ± or bifurcation point).

```
Nest[q[2], 0.25, 100]
```

```
0.5
```

```
Nest[q[2], 0.75, 100]
```

```
0.5
```

```
lis2 = NestList[q[2.5], 0.5, 20];
ListPlot[
  lis2, PlotJoined -> True, PlotRange -> {0.5, 0.7}];
```

```
lis3 = NestList[q[3], 0.75, 100];
BarChart[lis3, Ticks -> {None, Automatic}];
```

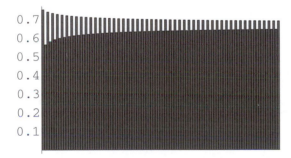

(4) If $3 < u < 3.56994^{\circ}$, then there is a periodic cycle.

The theory is quite subtle. For a fuller explanation, the reader may consult *Encounters with Chaos*, by Denny Gulick (McGraw-Hill, 1992), Section 1.5. In fact there is a sequence

$$u_0 = 3 < u_1 = 1 + \sqrt{6} < u_2 < u_3 < ^{\circ} \quad < 4,$$

such that between u_0 and u_1 there is a cycle of period 2; between u_1 and u_2 there is a cycle of period 4; and in general, between u_k and u_{k+1} there is a cycle of period 2^{k+1}. In fact, one knows that, at least for small k, one has the approximation $u_{k+1} \approx 1 + \sqrt{3 + u_k}$. So

```
u1 = N[1 + Sqrt[6]]
```

3.44949

```
u2approx = 1 + √(3 + u1) // N
```

3.53958

This explains the oscillatory behavior we saw in the last of the original four examples (with $u_0 < u = 3.4 < u_1$). Here is the behavior for $u_1 < u = 3.5 < u_2$. **BarChart** is particularly effective here for spotting the cycle of order 4.

```
lis4 = NestList[q[3.5], 0.75, 100];
BarChart[lis4, Ticks -> {None, Automatic}];
```

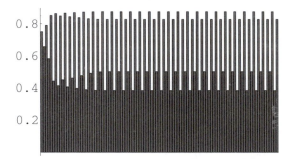

(5) There is a value $u < 4$ beyond which ± chaos!

It is possible to prove that the sequence u_k tends to a limit u_∞. The value of u_∞, sometimes called the *Feigenbaum parameter*, is approximately 3.56994° . Let's see what happens if we use a value of u between the Feigenbaum parameter and 4.

```
lis5 = NestList[q[3.7], 0.75, 100];
ListPlot[
 lis5, PlotJoined -> True, PlotRange -> {0.2, 1}];
```

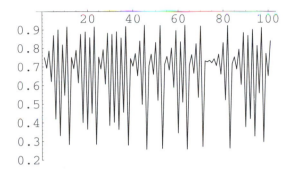

This is an example of what mathematicians call a *chaotic* phenomenon! It is not random ± the sequence was generated by a precise fixed mathematical procedure, but the results manifest no discernible pattern. Chaotic phenomena are unpredictable, but with modern methods (including computer analysis), mathematicians have been able to identify certain patterns of behavior in chaotic phenomena. For example, the last figure suggests the possibility of unstable periodic cycles and other recurring phenomena. Indeed a great deal of information is known. The aforementioned book by Gulick is a fine reference, as well as the source of an excellent bibliography on the subject.

CHEMICAL REACTIONS

We will study a standard kind of chemical reaction, model it with a differential equation, and use Mathematica to describe the eventual outcome of the reaction. Typically, two or more substances combine to form one or more new substances. Suppose two chemicals combine to form a compound C. Start with A grams of the first chemical and B grams of the second. We will denote by $x(t)$ the amount of the new compound after t minutes. We observe that the reaction between the two chemicals is such that the proportion $A : B$ of chemicals used in forming C is $u : 1 - u$, where $0 < u < 1$. For example, $u = 1/3$ means that for every gram of the first chemical, 2 grams of the second is required. The basic mathematical model of the reaction stipulates that the rate at which the amount $x(t)$ is changing is proportional to the product of the residual amounts of the two chemicals still present. The rate of change of $x(t)$ is its derivative $x'(t)$. Since it takes $u\, x(t)$ grams of the first chemical and $(1 - u)\, x(t)$ grams of the second to produce $x(t)$ grams of the new substance, we can express the model mathematically by the differential equation

$$x'(t) = k(A - u\, x(t))(B - (1 - u)\, x(t)).$$

The constant of proportionality k is not known at the outset but can be determined by measurement, as we shall see. Let's set Mathematica loose on the equation.

```
sol = DSolve[{x'[t] ==
    k * (A - u * x[t]) (B - (1 - u) * x[t]), x[0] == 0},
  x[t], t]
```

$$\left\{\left\{x[t] \to -\frac{A\,B\,(E^{Akt} - E^{Aktu+Bktu})}{-A\,E^{Akt} + A\,E^{Akt}\,u + B\,E^{Aktu+Bktu}\,u}\right\}\right\}$$

We used the initial condition $x(0) = 0$, since we assume there are no grams of C initially. Next we extract a function:

```
f[t_, A_, B_, u_, k_] = x[t] /. First[sol]
```

$$-\frac{A\,B\,(E^{Akt} - E^{Aktu+Bktu})}{-A\,E^{Akt} + A\,E^{Akt}\,u + B\,E^{Aktu+Bktu}\,u}$$

Now let us look at a couple of concrete examples.

■ Example 1

Suppose that 50 grams of the first substance and 32 grams of the second are present initially. Suppose also that it takes 4 grams of the latter for each gram of the former in the reaction. Finally, suppose we measure 30 grams of C after 10 minutes. Then we can use this data to solve for the coefficient of proportionality k.

```
coeff = FindRoot[f[10, 50, 32, 0.2, k] == 30,
   {k, 0.005}, MaxIterations -> 20]
```

$\{k \rightarrow 0.00374542\}$

(Note: we had to increase the default number of iterations in **FindRoot** to do the analysis.)

 Now we define a specific function corresponding to this data, check that it has the correct value for $t = 10$, compute its long-term behavior, plot it, and compute the point where the reaction is 99 percent finished.

```
f1[t_] =
  f[t, 50, 32, 0.2, k /. First[coeff]] // FullSimplify
```

$$40. + \frac{1}{0.0047619 - 0.0297619 \, E^{0.125846\,t}}$$

```
f1[10] //N
```

$30.$

```
Limit[f1[t], t -> Infinity]
```

$40.$

```
Plot[f1[t], {t, 0, 40}, PlotRange -> {0, 40},
  AxesLabel -> {"Time", "Quantity"}];
```

```
FindRoot[f1[t] == 0.99*40, {t, 35}]
```

$\{t \rightarrow 35.2233\}$

■ Example 2

Now assume that there are 50 grams of the first substance and 80 grams
of the second. Assume $u = 0.6$; that is, it takes 3 grams of the former for
each 2 grams of the latter for the reaction to proceed. Once again,
assume that 30 grams of the new substance is present after 30 minutes.
We carry out the same analysis.

```
coeff2 = FindRoot[f[10, 50, 80, 0.6, k] == 30,
   {k, 0.005}, MaxIterations -> 20]
```

$\{k \to 0.00101346\}$

```
f2[t_] =
 f[t, 50, 80, 0.6, k /. First[coeff2]] // FullSimplify
```

$$83.3333 + \frac{1}{0.00857143 - 0.0205714\,E^{0.0283768\,t}}$$

```
f2[10] // N
```

$30.$

```
lim2 = Limit[f2[t], t -> Infinity]
```

83.3333

```
Plot[f2[t], {t, 0, 100}, PlotRange -> {0, 82},
 AxesLabel -> {"Time", "Quantity"}];
```

```
FindRoot[f2[t] == 0.99 * lim2, {t, 74}]
```

$\{t \rightarrow 143.543\}$

The picture looks flat around $t = 80$ minutes, but this reaction is slower than the first ± it takes 143.543 minutes to complete 99 percent of the process.

THE 360   PENDULUM

Normally we think of a pendulum as a weight suspended by a flexible string or cable, so that it may swing back and forth. Another type of pendulum consists of a weight attached by a light (but inflexible) rod to an axle, so that it can swing through larger angles, even making a 360 rotation if given enough velocity.

Though it is not precisely correct in practice, we often assume that the magnitude of the frictional forces that eventually slow the pendulum to a halt is proportional to the velocity of the pendulum. Assume also that the length of the pendulum is 1 meter, the weight at the end of the pendulum has mass 1 kg, and the coefficient of friction is 0.5. In that case, the equations of motion for the pendulum are as follows:

```
pendeqns =
  {x'[t] == y[t], y'[t] == -0.5 y[t] - 9.81 Sin[x[t]]};
```

Here t represents time in seconds, x represents the angle of the pendulum from the vertical in radians (so that $x = 0$ is the rest position), y represents the velocity of the pendulum in radians per second, and 9.81 is approximately the acceleration due to gravity in meters per second squared. Now we create a function that will numerically find the solution as a function of t for a given initial angle $x0$ and initial velocity $y0$.

```
pendsol[t_, x0_, y0_] := {x[t], y[t]} /.
    First[NDSolve[{pendeqns, x[0] == x0, y[0] == y0},
        {x[t], y[t]}, {t, 0, 20}]]
```

Here is a phase portrait of the solution with $x0 = 0$ and $y0 = 5$. This is a graph of x versus y as a function of t.

```
ParametricPlot[Evaluate[pendsol[t, 0, 5]],
    {t, 0, 20}, PlotRange -> All];
```

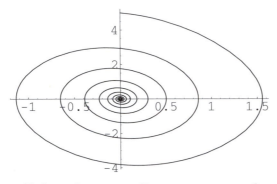

Recall that the x coordinate corresponds to the angle of the pendulum and the y coordinate corresponds to its velocity. Starting at (0, 5), as t increases we follow the curve as it spirals clockwise toward (0, 0). The angle oscillates back and forth, but with each swing it gets smaller until the pendulum is virtually at rest by the time $t = 20$. Meanwhile the velocity oscillates as well, taking its maximum value during each oscillation when the pendulum is in the middle of its swing (the angle is near zero) and crossing zero when the pendulum is at the end of its swing. Next we increase the initial velocity to 10.

```
ParametricPlot[Evaluate[pendsol[t, 0, 10]],
  {t, 0, 20}, PlotRange -> All];
```

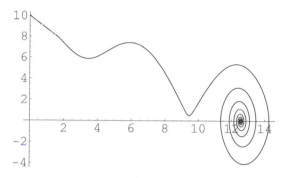

This time the angle increases to over 14 radians before the curve spirals inward to a point near (12.5, 0). More precisely, it spirals toward $(4\pi, 0)$, because 4π radians represents the same position for the pendulum as 0 radians does. The pendulum has swung overhead and made two complete revolutions before beginning its damped oscillation toward its rest position. The velocity at first decreases but then rises after the angle passes through π, as the pendulum passes the upright position and gains momentum. The pendulum has just enough momentum to swing through the upright position once more at the angle 3π.

Now suppose we want to find, to within 0.1, the minimum initial velocity required to make the pendulum, starting from its rest position, swing overhead once. It will be useful to be able to see the solutions corresponding to several different initial velocities on one graph. We define a function that will draw the solutions corresponding to initial velocities *v0* to *v1* in increments of *vinc*.

```
portrait[v0_, v1_, vinc_] := ParametricPlot[Evaluate[
   Table[pendsol[t, 0, y0], {y0, v0, v1, vinc}]],
   {t, 0, 20}, PlotRange -> All, PlotPoints -> 100]
```

First we consider the integer velocities 5 to 10.

```
portrait[5, 10, 1];
```

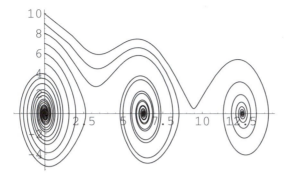

Initial velocities 5, 6, 7 are not large enough for the angle to increase past π, but initial velocities 8, 9, 10 are enough to make the pendulum swing overhead. Let's see what happens between 7 and 8.

```
portrait[7, 8, 0.2];
```

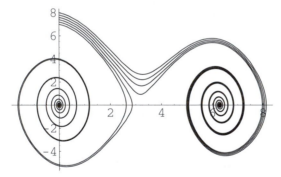

We see that the cutoff is somewhere between 7.2 and 7.4. Let's make one more refinement.

```
portrait[7.2, 7.4, 0.05];
```

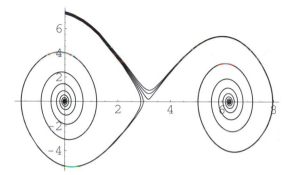

We conclude that the minimum velocity needed is somewhere between 7.25 and 7.3.

Chapter 7

Mathematica and the Web

You can use Mathematica with the World Wide Web in a number of different ways. You can prepare documents and graphics in Mathematica and make them available for others on a Web server. You can also look up information about Mathematica on the Web. In this chapter, we'll explain how to prepare Mathematica Notebooks for the Web and point you to some useful Web sites.

Creating Documents for the Web

You can put a Notebook on the Web in two different formats. By saving the Notebook in the HyperText Markup Language (HTML), you can make it available for viewing by anyone with a Web browser. You can also put Notebooks directly on the Web in their native Mathematica format. These Notebooks are then available as interactive documents to anyone who has access to a working copy of Mathematica and a properly configured Web browser.

Which format should you use? It depends on your goals. You will reach a much wider audience if you make your Notebook available as an HTML document. However, your viewers will only be able to look at a static copy of the document. If you want people to be able to interact with the document, then you must make it available as a live Notebook.

Saving as HTML

You can save a Notebook in HTML format in order to make it available on the World Wide Web. You must already have a Web server available to you in order for others to view your Notebook. It will not look exactly the same as it does in your Mathematica session, but it will be very similar.

To save your Notebook as HTML, select **File : Save as Special**...: **HTML**. In the dialog box, be sure to type in a file name that ends in ".htm" or ".html". (Mathematica does not add the file extension automatically.) If you type, for example, `mynb.htm`, then this file will be created along with auxiliary files

140

named `mynbgr1.gif`, `mynbgr2.gif`, *etc*. These files contain the graphics from your Notebook. To put your Notebook on the World Wide Web, you must copy all of these files to the appropriate directory for your system. (For instance, if you have your own home page, then you can use its directory.)

Native Mathematica Format

You can also put your Notebook on the World Wide Web in its native format. This will allow others with Mathematica both to view and to interact with your Notebook. People who do not have Mathematica can download a free program called MathReader from `http://www.wolfram.com/mathreader` for read-only access to your Notebook. However, for point-and-click access they will have to configure their World Wide Web browsers appropriately.

Preparing Notebooks for the Web

Mathematica Notebook files are generally quite large, so you may want to take measures to reduce the size of a Notebook that you are planning to post on the Web. The easiest way to reduce the size of a Notebook is to delete all output (including graphics) by selecting **Kernel**:**Delete All Output**. Then save the Notebook. Deleting the output will generally reduce the size of the Notebook by a factor of 10–20, and in some cases by a factor of 100 or more. Anyone with a copy of Mathematica on a computer can download the Notebook and then evaluate it to see the output.

In addition, you might want to make the evaluated Notebook available so that someone with only the MathReader program can download the larger Notebook with output and graphics.

For example, if you have a Notebook called "Sample.nb", then you could delete the output and save it as "Samplesmall.nb". You would then insert the following lines in your HTML file:

```
Here is a Mathematica Notebook in both an
<A HREF="Samplesmall.nb">unevaluated version</A>
(21 Kilobytes), and an
<A HREF="Sample.nb">evaluated version</A>
(336 Kilobytes).
```

Graphics

You can use Mathematica to produce graphics for inclusion in other Web pages. If you are comfortable with the procedure described earlier, then you can use it as a quick and dirty way to produce graphics files. Start by entering the commands that produce the graphic you want in a Notebook. Save the Notebook as an HTML file. Now find the corresponding graphic file with a ".gif" extension, and copy it to your Web site.

A better method for exporting individual graphics from Notebooks is to use the Display command. Enter the commands that produce the graphic; make certain that you assign a name to the graphic. For example, suppose that you have created a Mathematica graphic named myplot. Then the command

```
Display["myplot.gif", myplot, "GIF"]
```

will save the graphic in a file called "myplot.gif" in the GIF format, which is the most common graphics format on the Web. (You can use the online help to find out what other formats are available with the Display command.)

By default, an image created by the Display command will be four inches wide. You can change the width with the ImageSize option. The value of this option specifies the width of the figure in printer's points. Since there are 72 points to an inch, using the option ImageSize -> 144 would produce a file containing a graphic whose natural width is two inches.

Finally, here is a simple way to transfer a graphic from Mathematica to another application. In your Notebook, click on the graphic you want to export. From the **Edit** menu, select **Copy As**, then choose an appropriate format for the graphic. This will place the graphic on the clipboard. From there, you can paste it into another application.

VRML

The acronym VRML stands for the "Virtual Reality Markup Language". VRML is a three-dimensional version of HTML, which allows you to create interactive three-dimensional scenes with hyperlinks to other VRML and HTML documents. The central location on the World Wide Web for information about VRML is the repository at http://www.sdsc.edu/vrml/, which is maintained by the San Diego Supercomputer Center. The repository contains a comprehensive listing of VRML products, including standalone VRML browsers and viewers that plug into most standard Web browsers.

You can use Mathematica to create three-dimensional objects that can be viewed by VRML browsers. This procedure is slightly more complicated than the procedure to create GIF files, because Mathematica does not directly provide the capability to export three-dimensional graphics as VRML files.

Start by producing a three-dimensional graphics object using an appropriate Mathematica graphics command (such as Plot3D). For this example, we will assume that you have named this object **myplot**. Now enter the commands

```
<<Utilities`DXF`
WriteDXF["myplot.dxf", Graphics3D[myplot]]
```

These commands will load the DXF package and create a file called "myplot.dxf" that contains the three-dimensional object in DXF format. (This is the native format of the AutoCAD program.) Now you need a "graphics translator" that can convert DXF files to VRML format. (The San Diego Supercomputer Center's VRML Repository has a list of graphics translators.) One that works well (and has the added virtue of being free) is called wcvt2pov. After starting wcvt2pov, select **File** : **Open** and locate your DXF file. Then select **File** : **Save As**... and specify VRML as the format of the new file.

Configuring Your Web Browser

In this section, we explain how to configure the most popular Web browsers to display Mathematica Notebooks.

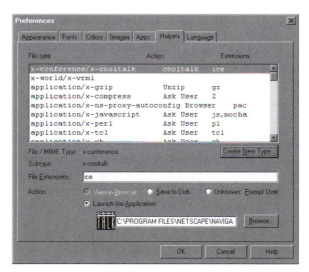

Figure 7-1: Netscape Preferences dialog box

Microsoft Internet Explorer

If Mathematica is installed on your Windows 95 computer then Internet Explorer should automatically know how to open Mathematica Notebooks.

Netscape Navigator in Windows 95

To configure Netscape Navigator to open Mathematica Notebooks, do the following:

1. Select **Options** : **General Preferences**... in the Netscape menu bar.

2. Select the **Helpers** panel in the "Preferences" dialog box (Figure 7-1).

3. Click **Create New Type**. In the "Configure New Mime Type" dialog box, type "application" on the first line, and "mathematica" on the second line (Figure 7-2). Then click "OK".

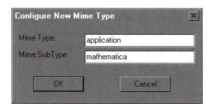

Figure 7-2: Configure New Mime Type dialog box

4. In the "File Extensions" box of the "Preferences" dialog box, type "ma,nb". This will allow you to open both new and old-style Notebooks.

5. Click the "Browse" button in the lower right-hand corner. In the dialog panel that appears, click on folders until you find your copy of Mathematica and select "Mathematica.exe". Then click "OK".

6. Finally, check the "Preferences" panel to make sure the new entry looks like the entry in Figure 7-3. Then click "OK".

Netscape on UNIX Systems

Look in your home directory for a file called ".mime.types". Open this file with an editor (or create a new file called ".mime.types" if you don't already have one). Add the line

```
application/mathematica     ma nb
```
and then save the file.

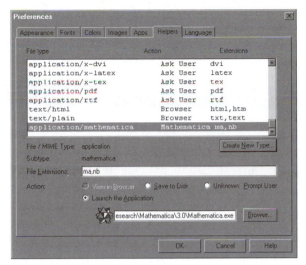

Figure 7-3: Netscape Preferences dialog box

Now check to see whether you have a file called ".mailcap". Open it with an editor (or create a file called ".mailcap" if you don't already have one). Add the line

```
application/mathematica; mathematica %s
```

to the file. If the command for starting Mathematica on your system is something other than "mathematica", then you'll have to replace the word "mathematica" to the right of the semicolon with the name of the appropriate command.

The mime type and mailcap definitions can also be set up on a systemwide basis; consult your system administrator.

Web Sites About Mathematica

The foremost World Wide Web site containing information about Mathematica is, of course, the site maintained by Wolfram Research, Inc., the company that produces the program. Their site at

```
http://www.wolfram.com/
```

contains information about product upgrades, answers to frequently asked questions, and an extensive list of related books and products. Of particular interest is the list of specialized packages that you can order to accompany Mathematica, which is located at `http://www.wolfram.com/applications/`

There is also an extensive collection of free packages, programs, and other information located at

`http://www.wolfram.com/mathsource/`

Finally, their page on product support and training at

`http://www.wolfram.com/user_support`

has useful information.

The authors of this primer maintain a Web site at

`http://www.math.umd.edu/schol/primer`

This site contains the application Notebooks from Chapter 6 and the Notebook solutions to the practice sets.

For an extensive list of sites where Mathematica is used and discussed (such as `http://othello.ma.ic.ac.uk/wwwmath/`, home of the WWWMath Discussion Group), enter "Mathematica" into your favorite Web search engine.

Chapter 8

Troubleshooting

In this chapter, we offer advice for dealing with some common problems that you may encounter. We also list and describe the most common mistakes that people make.

Common Problems

Problems manifest themselves in various ways: totally unexpected or plainly wrong output appears; Mathematica produces an error message; Mathematica refuses to process an input line; something that worked earlier stops working; or, worst of all, the computer freezes. Fortunately, these problems are often caused by several easily identifiable and correctable mistakes. What follows is a description of some common problems, together with a presentation of likely causes, suggested solutions, and illustrative examples. We also refer to places in the book where related issues are discussed.

Here is a list of the problems:

- Wrong or unexpected output
- Mathematica echoes the input line
- Syntax error
- Spelling error
- Error message involving an equation
- Multiple error messages when plotting
- A Notebook fails to evaluate
- Computer won't respond

Problem: Wrong or Unexpected Output

There are many possible causes for this problem, but they are likely to be among the following:

147

CAUSE: Forgetting to clear values.

SOLUTION: **Clear variables before using them, especially in a long session.**

☞ *See* Clearing Values *in Chapter 4.*

EXAMPLE:

Suppose you type

```
In[1]:=  x = 4

Out[1]=  4
```

Then, perhaps much later in the session, or in a different Notebook, you type

```
In[2]:=  g[x_] := x^2 + x

In[3]:=  g[1]

Out[3]=  2

In[4]:=  g[x]

Out[4]=  20
```

The function g was defined with delayed evaluation. Therefore $g(1)$ gives the correct answer. But $g(x)$ gives the wrong answer because Mathematica thinks $x = 4$.

CAUSE: Not keeping track of In/Out numbering.

SOLUTION: **Always assign a name to output that you intend to use.**

If you decide at some point in a session that you wish to refer to prior output that was unnamed, then go back, enter a name, and execute the command line again.

☞ *See* Referring to Previous Output *in Chapter 2.*

EXAMPLE:

```
In[6]:=  a - b

Out[6]=  a - b
```

```
In[5]:=  a + b
```

Out[5]= $a + b$

```
In[7]:=  Expand[%^2]
```

Out[7]= $a^2 - 2ab + b^2$

If you look closely at the line numbering, you'll see that the % in the `Expand` command refers to `In[6]`, which is `a - b`. The line just above the `Expand` is labeled `In[5]`. What happened is that the user, after entering `a + b`, then reentered the line containing `a - b`. Thus, the result of `In[7]` was to square `a - b` instead of `a + b`. Better practice would be to do the following:

```
In[8]:=  z = a + b;
         Expand[z^2]
```

Out[8]= $a^2 + 2ab + b^2$

CAUSE: Improper use of built-in functions.

SOLUTION: **Always use the names of built-in functions exactly as Mathematica specifies them; always enclose variables in brackets, not parentheses.**

☞ *See* Built-in Functions *in Chapter 2*

EXAMPLE:

The natural logarithm function in Mathematica is `Log[x]`. All of the following are wrong: `Log x`, `Logx`, `Log(x)`, or `Ln[x]`. So

```
In[9]:=  N[Log 3]
```

Out[9]= $3 . \text{Log}$

```
In[10]:=  N[Log3]
```

Out[10]= $\text{Log}3$

```
In[11]:=  N[Log(3)]
```

Out[11]= $3 . \text{Log}$

In[12]:= **N[Ln[3]]**

Out[12]= $\text{Ln}[3.]$

Mathematica interpreted the first and third inputs as the number 3 times the variable named **Log**, it interpreted the second input as the variable **Log3**, and it interpreted the fourth input as the unknown function **Ln** evaluated at 3.

CAUSE: Improperly concatenating variables.

SOLUTION: **Always use the multiplication sign rather than relying on a space to indicate multiplication.**

EXAMPLE:

xy is a variable named xy, whereas **x y** or **x*y** means x *times* y.

In[13]:= **Solve[x + 2xy + y == 0, x]**

Out[13]= $\{\{x \to -2xy - y\}\}$

In[14]:= **Solve[x + 2x*y + y == 0, x]]**

Out[14]= $\left\{\left\{x \to -\dfrac{y}{1 + 2y}\right\}\right\}$

In the first input, Mathematica interpreted the symbol **xy** as a distinct variable, not as the product of **x** and **y**.

CAUSE: Improper use of arithmetic symbols.

SOLUTION: **Use parentheses liberally and correctly when entering arithmetic or algebraic expressions.**

EXAMPLE:

Mathematica, like any calculator, first exponentiates, then divides and multiplies, and finally adds and subtracts, unless a different order is specified by using parentheses. So if you attempt to input the expression $a^{2/3} + b(u+v) - c/(2d)$ by typing

In[15]:= **a^2/3 + b * u + v - c/2d**

Out[15]= $\dfrac{a^2}{3} - \dfrac{cd}{2} + bu + v$

the expression Mathematica produces is not what you intended because **a** is raised to the power 2 before the division by 3, **b** is multiplied by **u** before the addition of **v**, and **c** is divided by 2 before the multiplication by **d**. Here is the correct input:

In[16]:= **a^(2/3) + b(u + v) - c/(2d)**

Out[16]= $a^{2/3} - \dfrac{c}{2d} + b(u + v)$

Problem: Mathematica Echoes the Input Line

CAUSE: Mathematica cannot carry out the requested computation.

SOLUTION: **Try a different approach.**

You may be able to try an alternate command, or load a special package, or even augment the original command with an option.

EXAMPLE:

In[17]:= **Integrate[Exp[-x^4 + x^3, {x, 0 1}]**

Out[17]= $\displaystyle\int_{0}^{1} E^{x^3-x^4} dx$

Mathematica cannot compute the definite integral. It returns the input line – in prettier format, but unevaluated. In this case, a numerical integration is an appropriate alternative.

In[18]:= **NIntegrate[Exp[-x^4 + x^3],{x, 0, 1}]**

Out[18]= 1.05204

CAUSE: Using a command from a Mathematica package before the package has been loaded.

SOLUTION: **Use the Remove command to remove the command you used before loading the package; then load the package and proceed.**

☞ *See* Packages *in Chapter 4.*

EXAMPLE:

In[19]:= **ImplicitPlot[x^2 - y^2 == 1, {x, -2, 2}]**

Out[19]= $\text{ImplicitPlot}[x^2 - y^2 == 1, \{x, -2, 2\}]$

In[20]:= **Remove[ImplicitPlot]**

In[21]:= **<<Graphics`ImplicitPlot`**

In[22]:= **ImplicitPlot[x^2 - y^2 == 1, {x, -2, 2}];**

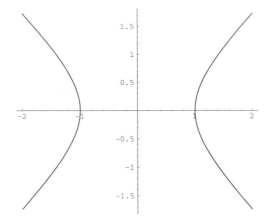

Problem: Syntax Error

CAUSE: Mismatched braces or brackets.

SOLUTION: **Look carefully at the input line to find a missing or an extra delimiter.**
Mathematica usually catches this kind of mistake. Mathematica beeps when
you type a right delimiter that does not have a matching left delimiter, or it
refuses to accept an input line after you press SHIFT+ENTER.

EXAMPLE:

```
In[23]:= Solve[{x + y == 2, x - y == 4, {x, y}]

         Syntax::bktmcp: Expression "{x + y == 2, x - y == 4,
           {x, y}" has no closing "}".

In[24]:= D[(x - y)*x + y), x]

         Syntax::bktmop: Expression "D[(x - y)* x + y), x]" has
           no opening "[".
```

In the first case Mathematica does not beep until you type the right bracket.
However, what is missing is a right brace after the 4. In the second case,
Mathematica beeps after you type both the right parenthesis and the right
bracket. Note that it incorrectly diagnoses the problem.

CAUSE: Improper use of arithmetic symbols.

SOLUTION: **When you encounter a syntax error, review your input line carefully for
mistakes in typing.**

EXAMPLE:

If the user, intending to compute 2 times -4, inadvertently switches the symbols, the result is

```
In[25]:= 2 - * 4

        Syntax::tsntxi: "*4" is incomplete; more input is
        needed.
```

Problem: Spelling Error

CAUSE: Using lowercase instead of uppercase letters in Mathematica commands or misspelling the command.

SOLUTION: **Fix the spelling.**

For example, Mathematica does not recognize **Findroot** or **findroot**; the correct command is **FindRoot**.

EXAMPLE:

```
In[26]:= Findroot[Cos[x] == x, {x, 1}]

        General::spell1: Possible spelling error: new symbol
        name "Findroot" is similar to existing symbol
        "FindRoot".

Out[26]= Findroot[Cos[x] == x, {x, 1}]
```

Problem: Error Message Involving an Equation

CAUSE: Typing the wrong kind of equal sign.

SOLUTION: **Use == for equations, and = or := for assigning variables or defining functions.**

☞ *See both* Names and Assignments *and* Solving Equations *in Chapter 2, as well as* Equations vs. Assignments *in Chapter 4.*

EXAMPLE:

In[27]:= **eqn = x^2 + 2x + 1 = 0**

Set::write : Tag Plus in 1 + 2x + x^2 is Protected.

Out[27]= 0

In[28]:= **Solve[eqn, x]**

Solve::eqf 0 is not a well-formed equation.

Out[28]= $\text{Solve}[0, x]$

The second equal sign in the definition of **eqn** should have been double equal. The mistake caused Mathematica to attempt to set the quadratic expression equal to 0, thereby producing the first error message. Then **Solve** failed because **eqn** has been set to **0**, and is not an equation; Mathematica has nothing to solve. A more serious consequence of this mistake would ensue if the faulty equation were **x = 1**, as not only would **Solve** fail, but the variable **x** would be set equal to 1. This value would have to be explicitly cleared before proceeding. Be particularly wary of this mistake when using the **Solve** and **FindRoot** commands, which require an equation as one of their arguments.

Problem: Multiple Error Messages When Plotting

CAUSE: Omitting the **Evaluate** command inside a plotting command, especially when using **Table** inside the plotting command.

SOLUTION: **Use the Evaluate command when you use another command (like Table) inside a plotting command.**

EXAMPLE:

In[29]:= **Plot[Table[x^j, {j, 1, 3}], {x, 0, 1}];**

Plot::plnr: Table[x^j, {j, 1, 3}] is not a machine -
 size real number at x = 4.16666666666666607`*^-8.
Plot::plnr: Table[x^j, {j, 1, 3}] is not a machine -
 size real number at x = 0.0405669915729157892`.
Plot::plnr: Table[x^j, {j, 1, 3}] is not a machine -
 size real number at x = 0.0848087998593736713`.
General::stop: Further output of Plot::plnr
 will be suppressed during this calculation.

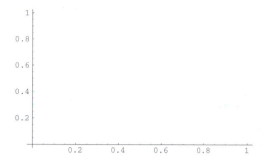

These imposing error messages indicate that you have tried to plot the wrong kind of object. In the command `Plot[stuff, {x, a, b}]`, Mathematica waits to evaluate `stuff` until after it substitutes numerical values for `x`. In the present case, Mathematica thinks `stuff` is an expression in `x`, which it expects to evaluate to a number. When it substitutes for `x` and evaluates, however, it gets a list of numbers:

```
In[30]:= Table[x^j, {j, 1, 3}] /. x -> 2
```

$$\text{Out[30]}= \{2, 4, 8\}$$

As another example, the command `Plot[D[x^3, x], {x, 0, 2}]` also fails. If you substitute 1 for `x` into `D[x^3, x]` before evaluating, you get `D[1^3, 1]`. This expression is meaningless because you cannot differentiate with respect to the "variable" 1.

☞ *For more information, see* Evaluate *in Chapter 5.*

CAUSE: Attempting to plot a function rather than an expression in a `Plot` command.

SOLUTION: **Make sure you plot the kinds of objects that the particular plotting command you are using requires.**

Check the syntax of your plotting command if you are unsure.

EXAMPLE:

```
In[31]:= h[x_] = x^2
```

$$\text{Out[31]}= x^2$$

```
In[32]:= Plot[h, {x, 0, 1}]
```

The resulting error messages (which are not shown here) are similar to those in Out[29].

Problem: A Previously Saved Notebook Evaluates Differently

One of the most frustrating problems you may encounter occurs when a previously saved Notebook, one which you are sure is in good shape, won't evaluate or evaluates incorrectly, when opened in a new session.

CAUSE: Change in the sequence of evaluation.

SOLUTION: **Organize your Notebook.**

It's hard to demonstrate an example succinctly, but there are two ways in which the sequence of evaluation can change. If you use the percent sign to refer to previous output, then there is a good chance that the In/Out numbering will be different when you reevaluate the Notebook. You should always assign names to output that you intend to reuse; don't rely on the percent sign.

☞ *See* Referring to Previous Output *in Chapter 2.*

There is another possibility. You may have jumped around in the Notebook in a previous session, clicking on Input cells and evaluating them out of order. If you did this, then the sequence of evaluation in the new session will be different. Check the Notebook to make sure that functions and variables are defined and packages are loaded before they are used.

☞ *See* Evaluating the Notebook *in Chapter 3 and* Packages *in Chapter 4.*

Problem: Computer Won't Respond

CAUSE: Mathematica is caught in a very large calculation, or some other calamity has occurred which has caused it to fail to respond.

EXAMPLE:

You'll know it when you see it.

☞ *See* Interrupting Calculations *in Chapter 1 for the solution.*

The Most Common Mistakes

The most common mistakes are all accounted for in the causes of the problems described earlier. But to help you prevent these mistakes, we compile them here in a single list to which you can refer periodically. Doing so will help you to establish "good Mathematica habits".

- Forgetting to clear values
- Not keeping track of In/Out numbering
- Improper use of built-in functions
- Improperly concatenating variables
- Improper use of arithmetic symbols
- Using a command from a Mathematica package before the package has been loaded
- Typing the wrong kind of equal sign
- Mismatched delimiters
- Omitting the `Evaluate` command inside a plotting command
- Plotting the wrong kind of object
- Using lowercase instead of uppercase letters in Mathematica commands or misspelling commands

Solutions to the Practice Sets

Practice Set A

■ Problem 1

(a)

```
7 + 4 + 2
```

13

(b)

```
3 ^ 321
```

14319332214339123434594355107434932207486745591177155415 ...
025682443731596064155042537750031640272113472226522148 45 ...
1089022111924704586692884400503449525120 3

(c)

Here are the first 25 digits of e^2:

```
N[E^2, 25]
```

7.389056098930650022723043

And here are the first 25 digits of π:

```
N[Pi, 25]
```

3.141592653589793238462643

(d)

```
N[{7 / 5, 141 / 100, 707 / 500, Sqrt[2]}]
```

{1.4, 1.41, 1.414, 1.41421}

The best of the three approximations to $\sqrt{2}$ is $\frac{707}{500}$.

■ Problem 2

(a)

```
N[Cos[0.1], 15]
```

0.995004165278026

(b)

```
N[Log[2], 15]
```

0.693147180559945

(c)

```
N[ArcTan[1 / 2], 15]
```

0.463647609000806

■ Problem 3

```
Factor[x^4 - y^4]
```

$(x - y) \ (x + y) \ (x^2 + y^2)$

■ Problem 4

```
? FactorInteger
```

FactorInteger[n] gives a list of the prime factors
    of the integer n, together with their exponents.

```
FactorInteger[123456789]
```

$\{\{3, 2\}, \{3607, 1\}, \{3803, 1\}\}$

This means that $123456789 = 3^2 * 3607 * 3803$.

■ Problem 5

(a)

```
Simplify[1 / (1 + 1 / (1 + 1 / x))]
```

$\dfrac{1 + x}{1 + 2 x}$

(b)

```
Cos[x]^2 - Sin[x]^2 // Simplify
```

$\text{Cos}[2 x]$

■ Problem 6

(a)

```
Solve[8 x + 3 == 0, x]
```

$\left\{\left\{x \to -\dfrac{3}{8}\right\}\right\}$

(b)

```
Solve[8 x + 3.0 == 0, x]
```

$\{\{x \to -0.375\}\}$

(c)

We'll solve the quadratic equation, then check the solutions.

```
quadraticsols = Solve[a * x^2 + b * x + c == 0, x]
```

$\left\{\left\{x \to \dfrac{-b - \sqrt{b^2 - 4\,a\,c}}{2\,a}\right\}, \left\{x \to \dfrac{-b + \sqrt{b^2 - 4\,a\,c}}{2\,a}\right\}\right\}$

Here's a way to check the solutions using the replacement operator:

```
a * x^2 + b * x + c /. quadraticsols
```

$$\left\{ c + \frac{b\left(-b - \sqrt{b^2 - 4\,a\,c}\,\right)}{2\,a} + \frac{\left(-b - \sqrt{b^2 - 4\,a\,c}\,\right)^2}{4\,a}, \right.$$

$$\left. c + \frac{b\left(-b + \sqrt{b^2 - 4\,a\,c}\,\right)}{2\,a} + \frac{\left(-b + \sqrt{b^2 - 4\,a\,c}\,\right)^2}{4\,a} \right\}$$

```
Simplify[%]
```

$\{0, 0\}$

Since the expression $a\,x^2 + b\,x + c$ evaluates to 0 when we substitute the values in **quadraticsols** for x, we have verified that the solutions in **quadraticsols** are correct.

(d)

```
Solve[{2 x + 3 y == 7, 3 x - y == 2}, {x, y}]
```

$\left\{\left\{x \rightarrow \dfrac{13}{11},\ y \rightarrow \dfrac{17}{11}\right\}\right\}$

(e)

```
cubicsols =
   Solve[{x^2 * y + 3 x - 2 y == 0, x + y == 3}, {x, y}]
```

$$\left\{\left\{y \to \frac{1}{2}\left(4 + \frac{8\, I\, 3^{1/6}}{\left(\frac{1}{2}\left(9 + I\sqrt{6063}\right)\right)^{1/3}} + \frac{\left(\frac{1}{2}\left(9 + I\sqrt{6063}\right)\right)^{1/3}}{3^{2/3}} - \right.\right.\right.$$

$$\left.\frac{I\left(9 + I\sqrt{6063}\right)^{1/3}}{2^{1/3}\, 3^{1/6}} + \frac{8}{\left(\frac{3}{2}\left(9 + I\sqrt{6063}\right)\right)^{1/3}}\right),\ x \to$$

$$\left.1 - \frac{\left(1 - I\sqrt{3}\right)\left(\frac{1}{2}\left(9 + I\sqrt{6063}\right)\right)^{1/3}}{2\, 3^{2/3}} - \frac{4\left(1 + I\sqrt{3}\right)}{\left(\frac{3}{2}\left(9 + I\sqrt{6063}\right)\right)^{1/3}}\right\},$$

$$\left\{y \to \frac{1}{2}\left(4 - \frac{8\, I\, 3^{1/6}}{\left(\frac{1}{2}\left(9 + I\sqrt{6063}\right)\right)^{1/3}} + \frac{\left(\frac{1}{2}\left(9 + I\sqrt{6063}\right)\right)^{1/3}}{3^{2/3}} + \right.\right.$$

$$\left.\frac{I\left(9 + I\sqrt{6063}\right)^{1/3}}{2^{1/3}\, 3^{1/6}} + \frac{8}{\left(\frac{3}{2}\left(9 + I\sqrt{6063}\right)\right)^{1/3}}\right),\ x \to$$

$$\left.1 - \frac{\left(1 + I\sqrt{3}\right)\left(\frac{1}{2}\left(9 + I\sqrt{6063}\right)\right)^{1/3}}{2\, 3^{2/3}} - \frac{4\left(1 - I\sqrt{3}\right)}{\left(\frac{3}{2}\left(9 + I\sqrt{6063}\right)\right)^{1/3}}\right\},$$

$$\left\{y \to \frac{1}{6}\left(12 - \frac{16\, 3^{2/3}}{\left(\frac{1}{2}\left(9 + I\sqrt{6063}\right)\right)^{1/3}} - 2^{2/3}\left(3\left(9 + I\sqrt{6063}\right)\right)^{1/3}\right),\right.$$

$$\left.x \to 1 + \frac{\left(\frac{1}{2}\left(9 + I\sqrt{6063}\right)\right)^{1/3}}{3^{2/3}} + \frac{8}{\left(\frac{3}{2}\left(9 + I\sqrt{6063}\right)\right)^{1/3}}\right\}\right\}$$

The solutions are rather complicated, because Mathematica is doing exact arithmetic, and the solutions involve cube roots. Note that there are three solutions. To check the solutions, we use the same method as in part (c).

```
Simplify[{x^2*y + 3x - 2y, x + y} /. cubicsols]
```

```
{{0, 3}, {0, 3}, {0, 3}}
```

To get a decimal approximation of the solutions, we can type one of the numbers in the equations as a decimal, as follows:

```
Solve[{x^2*y + 3x - 2y == 0, x + y == 3.0}, {x, y}]
```

```
{{y → -0.888969, x → 3.88897}, {y → 2.12525, x → 0.874754},
  {y → 4.76372, x → -1.76372}}
```

If we check these solutions, however, we'll see that they are only approximately correct.

```
Simplify[{x^2*y + 3x - 2y, x + y} /. %]
```

$\{\{-1.77636 \times 10^{-15}, 3.\}, \{4.44089 \times 10^{-16}, 3.\},$
$\quad \{1.77636 \times 10^{-15}, 3.\}\}$

As you can see, for each of the three approximate solutions, the expression $x^2 y + 3 x - 2 y$ evaluates to something very close to 0 (on the order of 10^{-15}); the expression $x + y$ evaluates to "3.", which means that it is equal to 3 up to 16 digits, the default precision used by Mathematica.

■ Problem 7

(a)

```
Plot[2x - 3, {x, -4, 4}];
```

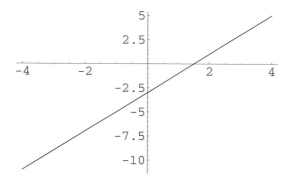

(b)

```
Plot[x^2 - x + 2, {x, -4, 4}];
```

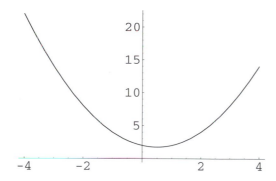

(c)

```
Plot[Sin[x], {x, 0, 20 Pi}];
```

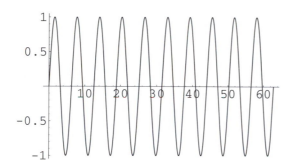

(d)

```
Plot[Tan[x/2], {x, -Pi, Pi}, PlotRange -> {-10, 10}];
```

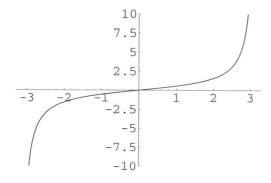

(e)

```
Plot[{Exp[(-x^2)/2], x^4 - x^2}, {x, -2, 2}];
```

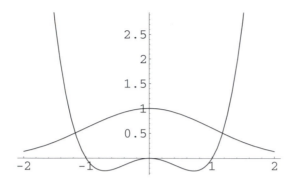

■ Problem 8

(a)

We start by defining the the function **f** to be the given polynomial expression.

```
f[x_] =
  x^6 - 21 x^5 + 175 x^4 - 735 x^3 + 1624 x^2 - 1764 x + 720
```

$720 - 1764\,x + 1624\,x^2 - 735\,x^3 + 175\,x^4 - 21\,x^5 + x^6$

(b)

```
f[0.5]
f[Sqrt[2]]
f[z^2]
```

162.422

$4676 - 3318\,\sqrt{2}$

$720 - 1764\,z^2 + 1624\,z^4 - 735\,z^6 + 175\,z^8 - 21\,z^{10} + z^{12}$

(c)

```
Table[f[x], {x, 0.1, 1, 0.1}] // TableForm
```
559.122
426.553
318.482
231.469
162.422
108.574
67.4607
36.9009
14.9737
0.

(d)

```
Factor[f[x]]
```
$(-6 + x)\ (-5 + x)\ (-4 + x)\ (-3 + x)\ (-2 + x)\ (-1 + x)$

(e)

```
Solve[f[x] == 0, x]
```
$\{\{x \to 1\},\ \{x \to 2\},\ \{x \to 3\},\ \{x \to 4\},\ \{x \to 5\},\ \{x \to 6\}\}$

Note that there are six distinct real roots.

(f)

```
Plot[f[x], {x, 0.9, 6.1}];
```

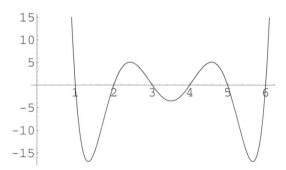

Practice Set B

■ Problem 1

Let's plot 2^x and x^4 and look for points of intersection. We plot 2^x in black and x^4 in gray, first over the interval $[-10, 10]$.

```
Plot[{x^4, 2^x}, {x, -10, 10},
 PlotStyle -> {GrayLevel[0.6], GrayLevel[0]}];
```

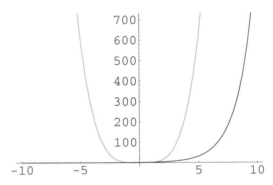

The vertical range is so large that the graph is not very informative, but we do learn that there are no points of intersection between 5 and 10 or -10 and -5. Let's focus on the interval between -5 and 5.

```
Plot[{x^4, 2^x}, {x, -5, 5},
 PlotStyle -> {GrayLevel[0.6], {}}];
```

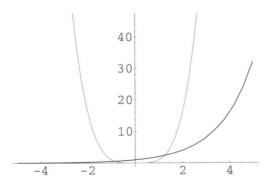

Now we can see that there are at least two intersections between -2 and 2. So let's focus on that interval.

```
Plot[{x^4, 2^x}, {x, -2, 2},
  PlotStyle -> {GrayLevel[0.6], {}}];
```

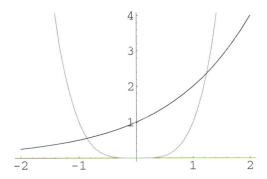

We see that there are points of intersection near −0.9 and 1.2. Are there any other points of intersection? To the left of 0, 2^x is always less than 1, whereas x^4 goes to infinity as x goes to -∞. On the other hand, both x^4 and 2^x go to infinity as x goes to ∞, so the graphs may cross again to the right of 0. Let's check.

```
Plot[{x^4, 2^x}, {x, 10, 20},
  PlotStyle -> {GrayLevel[0.6], {}}];
```

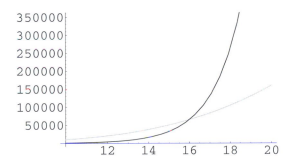

We see that they do cross again, near $x = 16$. If you know a little calculus, you can show that the graphs never cross again (by taking logarithms, for example), so we have found all the points of intersection. Now let's use the **FindRoot** command to find these points of intersection numerically. This command looks for a solution near a given starting point. To find the three different points of intersection we will have to use three different starting points. The preceding graphical analysis suggests appropriate starting points.

```
r1 = FindRoot[x^4 == 2^x, {x, -0.9}]
```

$\{x \rightarrow -0.861345\}$

```
r2 = FindRoot[x^4 == 2^x, {x, 1.2}]
```

$\{x \rightarrow 1.23963\}$

```
r3 = FindRoot[x^4 == 2^x, {x, 16}]
```

$\{x \rightarrow 16.\}$

Let's check that these "solutions" satisfy the equation.

```
x^4 - 2^x /. r1
```

1.76258×10^{-10}

```
x^4 - 2^x /. r2
```

6.38857×10^{-10}

```
x^4 - 2^x /. r3
```

$0.$

So $r1$ and $r2$ very nearly satisfy the equation, and $r3$ satisfies it exactly. It is easily seen that 16 is a solution. It is also interesting to try **Solve** on this equation.

```
sol = Solve[x^4 == 2^x, x]
```

InverseFunction::ifun :
  Warning: Inverse functions are being used. Values
    may be lost for multivalued inverses.

InverseFunction::ifun :
  Warning: Inverse functions are being used. Values
    may be lost for multivalued inverses.

InverseFunction::ifun :
  Warning: Inverse functions are being used. Values
    may be lost for multivalued inverses.

General::stop :
  Further output of InverseFunction::ifun will be
    suppressed during this calculation.

Solve::ifun : Inverse functions are being used by
    Solve, so some solutions may not be found.

$$\left\{\left\{x \to -\frac{4 \operatorname{ProductLog}\left[-\frac{\operatorname{Log}[2]}{4}\right]}{\operatorname{Log}[2]}\right\},\right.$$

$$\left\{x \to -\frac{4 \operatorname{ProductLog}\left[-\frac{1}{4} \, I \operatorname{Log}[2]\right]}{\operatorname{Log}[2]}\right\},$$

$$\left\{x \to -\frac{4 \operatorname{ProductLog}\left[\frac{1}{4} \, I \operatorname{Log}[2]\right]}{\operatorname{Log}[2]}\right\},$$

$$\left\{x \to -\frac{4 \operatorname{ProductLog}\left[\frac{\operatorname{Log}[2]}{4}\right]}{\operatorname{Log}[2]}\right\},$$

$$\left.\left\{x \to -\frac{4 \operatorname{ProductLog}\left[-1, -\frac{\operatorname{Log}[2]}{4}\right]}{\operatorname{Log}[2]}\right\}\right\}$$

Although we get a warning message, **Solve** finds five solutions. Let's examine them.

```
N[x /. sol[[1]]]
```

1.23963

```
N[x /. sol[[2]]]
```

$-0.160887 + 0.959105 \, I$

```
N[x /. sol[[3]]]
```
$-0.160887 - 0.959105 \, I$

```
N[x /. sol[[4]]]
```
-0.861345

```
N[x /. sol[[5]]]
```
16.

So we have two complex solutions, plus the three real solutions found previously. Only the real solutions correspond to points where the graphs intersect.

■ Problem 2

(a)

```
ContourPlot[3 y + y^3 - x^3, {x, -1, 1}, {y, -1, 1}];
```

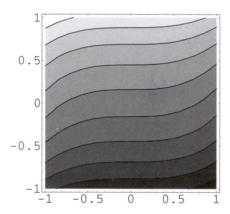

```
ContourPlot[3 y + y^3 - x^3, {x, -10, 10}, {y, -10, 10}];
```

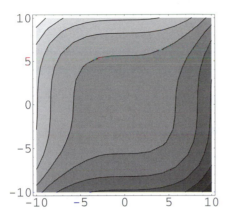

Here is a plot with more level curves:

```
ContourPlot[3 y + y^3 - x^3, {x, -10, 10},
  {y, -10, 10}, Contours -> 30];
```

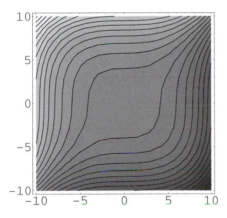

(b)

Now we use the options **Contours -> {5}** and **ContourShading ->
False**.

```
ContourPlot[3 y + y^3 - x^3, {x, -5, 5}, {y, -5, 5},
  Contours -> {5}, ContourShading -> False];
```

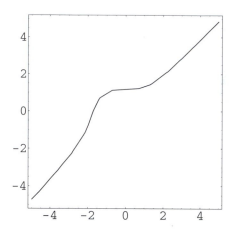

(c)

We note that $f(1, 1) = 0$, so the appropriate command to plot the level curve of f through the point $(1, 1)$ is

```
ContourPlot[y * Log[x] + x * Log[y], {x, 0.1, 2},
  {y, 0.1, 2}, Contours -> {0}, ContourShading -> False];
```

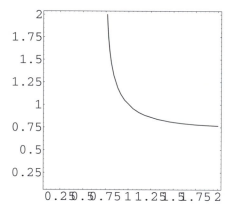

■ Problem 3

We find the derivatives of the given functions:

(a)

```
D[6 x^3 - 5 x^2 + 2 x - 3, x]
```

$2 - 10\, x + 18\, x^2$

(b)

```
D[(2 x - 1) / (x^2 + 1), x]
```

$-\dfrac{2\, x\,(-1 + 2\, x)}{(1 + x^2)^2} + \dfrac{2}{1 + x^2}$

Simplify[%]

$\dfrac{2 + 2\, x - 2\, x^2}{(1 + x^2)^2}$

(c)

```
D[Sin[3 x^2 + 2], x]
```

$6\, x \, \text{Cos}\,[2 + 3\, x^2]$

(d)

```
D[ArcSin[2 x + 3], x]
```

$\dfrac{2}{\sqrt{1 - (3 + 2\, x)^2}}$

(e)

```
D[Sqrt[1 + x^4], x]
```

$\dfrac{2\, x^3}{\sqrt{1 + x^4}}$

(f)

```
D[x^r, x]
```

$r\, x^{-1+r}$

(g)

```
D[ArcTan[x^2 + 1], x]
```

$\dfrac{2\, x}{1 + (1 + x^2)^2}$

■ Problem 4

The **Limit** command doesn't calculate two-sided limits; with the default option, it calculates the limit from the right, except for limits at infinity. So, if a two-sided limit is requested, we have to calculate both one-sided limits. Let's begin by reviewing the options to **Limit** using the online help.

Options[Limit]

{Analytic → False, Direction → Automatic}

? Direction

Direction is an option for Limit. With Direction -> 1, the limit is taken from below. With Direction -> -1, the limit is taken from above. Direction -> Automatic uses Direction -> -1 except for limits at Infinity, where it is equivalent to Direction -> 1.

We calculate a limit from the left with the option **Direction -> 1**.

(a)

Limit[Sin[x] / x, x -> 0, Direction -> 1]

1

Limit[Sin[x] / x, x -> 0]

1

The (two-sided) limit is 1.

(b)

Limit[(1 + Cos[x]) / (x + Pi), x -> -Pi, Direction -> 1]

0

Limit[(1 + Cos[x]) / (x + Pi), x -> -Pi]

0

(c)

```
Limit[x^2*Exp[-x], x -> Infinity]
```

0

(d)

```
Limit[1/(x - 1), x -> 1, Direction -> 1]
```

$-\infty$

(e)

```
Limit[Sin[1/x], x -> 0]
```

Interval[{-1, 1}]

This means that every real number in the interval between -1 and $+1$ is a "limit point" of $\sin(1/x)$ as x tends to zero. You can see why if you plot $\sin(1/x)$ on the interval $(0, 1]$.

```
Plot[Sin[1/x], {x, 0, 1}];
```

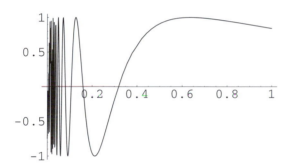

■ Problem 5

We compute the following integrals:

(a)

```
Integrate[Cos[x], {x, 0, Pi/2}]
```

1

(b)

`Integrate[x * Sin[x^2], x]`

$$-\frac{1}{2}\,\text{Cos}\,[x^2]$$

To check the indefinite integral, we just differentiate.

`D[-Cos[x^2] / 2, x]`

$$x\,\text{Sin}\,[x^2]$$

(c)

`Integrate[Sin[3 x] * Sqrt[1 - Cos[3 x]], x]`

$$-\frac{1}{3}\,\sqrt{1 - \text{Cos}\,[3\,x]}\,\left(-\frac{2}{3} + \frac{2}{3}\,\text{Cos}\,[3\,x]\right)$$

`D[%, x]`

$$\frac{2}{3}\,\sqrt{1 - \text{Cos}\,[3\,x]}\,\,\text{Sin}\,[3\,x] - \frac{\left(-\frac{2}{3} + \frac{2}{3}\,\text{Cos}\,[3\,x]\right)\,\text{Sin}\,[3\,x]}{2\,\sqrt{1 - \text{Cos}\,[3\,x]}}$$

`Simplify[%]`

$$\frac{4\,\text{Cos}\,[\frac{3\,x}{2}]\,\text{Sin}\,[\frac{3\,x}{2}]^3}{\sqrt{1 - \text{Cos}\,[3\,x]}}$$

`FullSimplify[%]`

$$\sqrt{1 - \text{Cos}\,[3\,x]}\,\,\text{Sin}\,[3\,x]$$

(d)

`Integrate[(x^2) * Sqrt[x + 4], x]`

$$\sqrt{4 + x}\,\left(\frac{1024}{105} - \frac{128\,x}{105} + \frac{8\,x^2}{35} + \frac{2\,x^3}{7}\right)$$

`D[%, x] // Simplify`

$$x^2\,\sqrt{4 + x}$$

(e)

`Integrate[Exp[-x^2], {x, -Infinity, Infinity}]`

$$\sqrt{\pi}$$

■ Problem 6

We approximate the following integrals using the **NIntegrate** command:

(a)

```
NIntegrate[Exp[Sin[x]], {x, 0, Pi}]
```

6.20876

(b)

```
NIntegrate[Sqrt[x^3 + 1], {x, 0, 1}]
```

1.11145

(c)

```
val = NIntegrate[Exp[-x^2], {x, -Infinity, Infinity}]
```

1.77245

Finally, we compare the numerical answer with the exact answer.

```
N[Sqrt[Pi] - val]
```

4.9257×10^{-10}

Thus the numerical approximation is good to 10 decimal places.

■ Problem 7

(a)

```
Plot3D[Sin[x] * Sin[y], {x, -10, 10}, {y, -10, 10},
 PlotPoints -> 50];
```

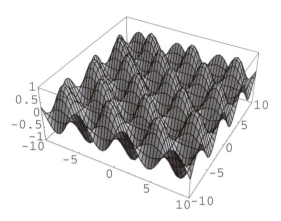

(b)

```
Plot3D[(x^2 + y^2) * (Cos[x^2 + y^2]), {x, -1, 1},
 {y, -1, 1}, PlotPoints -> 20];
```

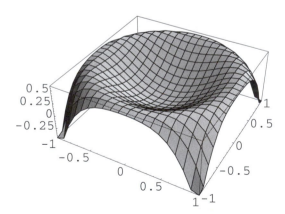

■ Problem 8

In this exercise, we illustrate three different approaches to drawing the unit sphere.

(a)

Our first approach is to do a parametric plot.

```
ParametricPlot3D[
  {Sin[phi] * Cos[theta], Sin[phi] * Sin[theta], Cos[phi]},
  {phi, 0, Pi}, {theta, 0, 2 * Pi}];
```

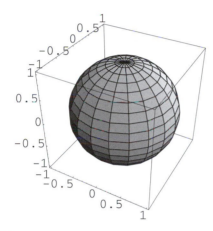

(b)

Our second approach is to use a contour plot. The **ContourPlot3D** command is in the **Graphics** package and must be loaded before we can use it.

<< Graphics`

We want to plot the contour of the function $x^2 + y^2 + z^2$ at level 1, so we type

```
ContourPlot3D[x^2 + y^2 + z^2, {x, -1, 1},
  {y, -1, 1}, {z, -1, 1}, Contours -> {1}];
```

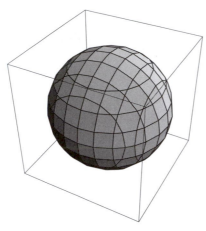

(c)

In our third approach we plot the upper hemisphere by considering it as the graph of the function $\sqrt{1 - x^2 - y^2}$.

```
Plot3D[Sqrt[1 - x^2 - y^2], {y, -1, 1}, {x, -1, 1}];
```

```
Plot3D::gval : Function value 0. + 1. I at grid point
   xi = 1, yi = 1 is not a real number.

Plot3D::gval : Function value 0. + 0.857143 I at
   grid point xi = 1, yi = 2 is not a real number.

Plot3D::gval : Function value 0. + 0.714286 I at
   grid point xi = 1, yi = 3 is not a real number.

General::stop : Further output of Plot3D::gval will
   be suppressed during this calculation.
```

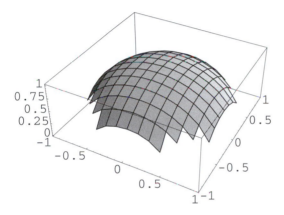

That didn't work very well. The problem is that we'd like to plot the graph of the function over the circular region $x^2 + y^2 < 1$, but in **Plot3D**, the region must be rectangular. Here's a technique to truncate the function outside the circular region: we use the **If** command to set the function to 0 outside the circular region.

? If

```
If[condition, t, f] gives t if condition evaluates to
   True, and f if it evaluates to False. If[condition, t,
   f, u] gives u if condition evaluates to neither
   True nor False.
```

```
Plot3D[If[x^2 + y^2 <= 1, Sqrt[1 - x^2 - y^2], 0],
  {y, -1, 1}, {x, -1, 1}, PlotPoints -> 20];
```

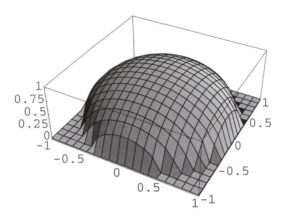

Not too bad, but still not as satisfactory as the results in (a) and (b).

■ Problem 9

The command **Series[f, {x, c, n}]** produces the Taylor polynomial of order n at c, with remainder expressed as $O((x-c)^n)$. The **Normal** command can be used to produce just the Taylor polynomial; this is useful if the Taylor polynomial is needed for a later calculation.

(a)

```
Series[Exp[x], {x, 0, 7}]
```

$$1 + x + \frac{x^2}{2} + \frac{x^3}{6} + \frac{x^4}{24} + \frac{x^5}{120} + \frac{x^6}{720} + \frac{x^7}{5040} + O[x]^8$$

```
p[x_] = Normal[%]
p[2]
```

$$1 + x + \frac{x^2}{2} + \frac{x^3}{6} + \frac{x^4}{24} + \frac{x^5}{120} + \frac{x^6}{720} + \frac{x^7}{5040}$$

$$\frac{155}{21}$$

(b)

```
Series[Sin[x], {x, 0, 5}]
```

$$x - \frac{x^3}{6} + \frac{x^5}{120} + O[x]^6$$

```
Series[Sin[x], {x, 0, 6}]
```

$$x - \frac{x^3}{6} + \frac{x^5}{120} + O[x]^7$$

(c)

```
Series[Sin[x], {x, 2, 6}]
```

$$\text{Sin}[2] + \text{Cos}[2] \ (x-2) - \frac{1}{2} \ \text{Sin}[2] \ (x-2)^2 -$$

$$\frac{1}{6} \ \text{Cos}[2] \ (x-2)^3 + \frac{1}{24} \ \text{Sin}[2] \ (x-2)^4 + \frac{1}{120} \ \text{Cos}[2] \ (x-2)^5 -$$

$$\frac{1}{720} \ \text{Sin}[2] \ (x-2)^6 + O[x-2]^7$$

(d)

```
Series[Tan[x], {x, 0, 7}]
```

$$x + \frac{x^3}{3} + \frac{2 x^5}{15} + \frac{17 x^7}{315} + O[x]^8$$

(e)

```
Series[Log[x], {x, 1, 5}]
```

$$(x-1) - \frac{1}{2} \ (x-1)^2 + \frac{1}{3} \ (x-1)^3 - \frac{1}{4} \ (x-1)^4 + \frac{1}{5} \ (x-1)^5 +$$

$$O[x-1]^6$$

(f)

```
Series[Erf[x], {x, 0, 9}]
```

$$\frac{2 x}{\sqrt{\pi}} - \frac{2 x^3}{3 \sqrt{\pi}} + \frac{x^5}{5 \sqrt{\pi}} - \frac{x^7}{21 \sqrt{\pi}} + \frac{x^9}{108 \sqrt{\pi}} + O[x]^{10}$$

■ Problem 10

(a)

```
Sum[i^2, {i, n}]
```

$$\frac{1}{6} n (1+n) (1+2n)$$

This is the well-known formula for the sum of the first n squares.

(b)

```
Sum[r^i, {i, 0, n}]
```

$$\frac{-1+r^{1+n}}{-1+r}$$

This is the sum of the geometric progression.

(c)

```
Sum[1/i^2, {i, 1, Infinity}]
```

$$\frac{\pi^2}{6}$$

(d)

```
Sum[(x^i)/i!, {i, 0, Infinity}]
```

$$E^x$$

The series is the Taylor series for e^x.

(d)

```
Sum[1/(z - i)^2, {i, -Infinity, Infinity}]
```

$$\pi^2 \operatorname{Csc}[\pi z]^2$$

■ Problem 11

We first make a table of the indicated plots.

```
Table[ParametricPlot[{4 * Cos[k * Pi / 8] + 0.5 * Cos[t],
   4 * Sin[k * Pi / 8] + 0.5 * Sin[t]},
  {t, 0, 2 Pi}, PlotRange -> {{-5, 5}, {-5, 5}},
  AspectRatio -> Automatic],
 {k, 0, 15}];
```

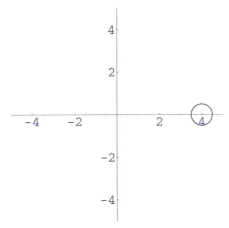

Next we double-click on the cell bracket for the group of plots, leaving only the first plot visible. Then we can animate the graphic by clicking on **Cell: Animate Selected Graphics** (though of course we cannot show that here).

Glossary

In this chapter, we list the most commonly used Mathematica objects in five categories: commands, options, functions, constants, and packages. Though Mathematica does not distinguish between commands and functions, it is convenient to think of a Mathematica function as we normally think of mathematical functions. A Mathematica function is something that can be evaluated or plotted; a command is something that manipulates data or expressions or that initiates a process.

We list each command, function, and option together with a short description of its effect, followed by one or more examples. Many Mathematica commands can appear in a number of different forms, because you can apply them to different kinds of objects. In our examples, we have illustrated the most commonly used forms of the commands. You can find a full description of all forms of a command by typing `?command`. Many commands also have numerous options; in this Glossary, we have only included some common options. You can get a list of all the options available for a command, together with their default values, by typing `??command`. You can also find information on each command and its options in the Help Browser.

This Glossary does not contain a comprehensive list of Mathematica commands and options. We have selected the commands and options that we feel are most important. You can find a comprehensive list in the Help Browser, which is shown in Figure G-1. The Help Browser is accessible from the **Help** menu by choosing **Help**.... To use the Help Browser effectively, you need to know that Mathematica makes a distinction between built-in objects (which are always available) and objects that are contained in packages. In this Glossary, we have intermingled the descriptions of built-in objects and packaged objects. When an object is stored in a package, our examples always show you how to load the object from the package before using it. To find built-in functions, options, commands, or constants in the Help Browser, you must select the "Built-in Functions" button at the top of the Help Browser. To find objects that are stored in packages, you must select the "Add-ons" button. In Figure G-1, we show the beginning of the help information on the **DescriptiveStatistics** package. We found this page by selecting "Standard Packages", then "Statistics", then "DescriptiveStatistics".

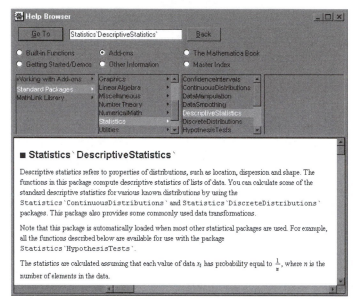

Figure G-1: The Help Browser

☞ *See* Online Help *in Chapter 3 for a description of the Help Browser.*

Mathematica Commands

Array   Uses a function to produce an array. Similar to **Table**, which uses an *expression* instead of a *function*. Compare the following:

```
Array[Exp, 11, 0]
Table[Exp[i], {i, 0, 10}]
```

BarChart   In the **Graphics`Graphics`** package. Generates a bar chart from the given data.

```
<<Graphics`Graphics`
BarChart[{1, 3, -1, 4}, {6, 2, 0, 1},
 BarLabels -> {"A", "B", "C", "D"} ]
```

BarChart3D   In the **Graphics`Graphics3D`** package. Generates a bar chart from a rectangular matrix of data.

```
<<Graphics`Graphics3D`
BarChart3D[{{1, 3}, {9, 2}}]
```

Clear   Clears values and definitions for variables and functions.

```
Clear[y]
Clear[x, y, f]
```

Collect   Collects the terms in an expression involving the same powers of a specified variable.

```
Collect[a*x^2 - b*x + x^2/c, x]
```

Composition   Represents the composition of functions.

```
f = Composition[Exp, #^2&]
Map[Composition[Exp, Sin], {1, 2, 3, 4}]
```

ContourPlot   Plots level curves of a function of two variables.

```
ContourPlot[x^3 + y^3, {x, -4, 4}, {y, -2, 2}]
```

ContourPlot3D   In the **Graphics** package. Plots level surfaces of an expression involving three variables.

```
<<Graphics`ContourPlot3D`
ContourPlot3D[x*y*z, {x, -1, 1}, {y, -1, 1},
 {z, 0, 1}]
```

D   Computes ordinary and partial derivatives of expressions. For functions, use a prime.

```
D[x^2, x]
D[g[t], t]
D[Sin[x], {x, 2}]
D[Exp[x/y], x, x, y]
Log´[x]
Cos´
```

DensityPlot   Similar to **ContourPlot**. Given an expression involving two variables, produces a shaded graph, with lighter colors corresponding to larger values of the expression.

```
DensityPlot[x^2 + y^2, {x, -2, 2}, {y, -2, 2}]
```

DiagonalMatrix   Produces a diagonal matrix with the elements of a given list along the diagonal.

```
DiagonalMatrix[{1, 2, 5, 4}] //MatrixForm
```

Det   Computes the determinant of a square matrix.

```
Det[{{1, 3, 4}, {2, 0, 6}, {i, j, k}}]
```

Do   Introduces a programming loop that repeatedly evaluates an expression.

```
total = 0
Do[total = total + i^2, {i, 1, 100}]
```

Dot   Multiplies vectors, matrices, and tensors. Usually written ".".

```
{1, 8, 7}.{2, 1, Pi}  (dot product of vectors)
{{2, 1}, {3, 5}}.{x, y}  (multiply a vector by a matrix)
{{2, 1}, {3, 5}}.DiagonalMatrix[1, 2]  (multiply matrices)
```

DSolve   Finds symbolic solutions for ordinary differential equations.

```
DSolve[y´[x] == x^2*y[x], y[x], x]
DSolve[{z´´[x] - x*z[x] == 0, z[0] == 1}, z[x], x]
DSolve[{x´[t] == x[t], y´[t] == -3x[t] +2y[t]},
  {x[t], y[t]}, t]
```

Eigensystem   Computes eigenvalues and eigenvectors of a square matrix. The output is a nested list, consisting of a list of eigenvalues, followed by a list of corresponding eigenvectors.

```
Eigensystem[{{1, 3}, {7, 2.3}}]
Eigensystem[{{i, j, k}, {3, 1, 5}, {2, 3, 7}}]
```

Eigenvalues   Computes eigenvalues of a square matrix.

```
Eigenvalues[{{Pi, 2}, {8, 3}}]
```

Eigenvectors   Computes eigenvectors of a square matrix.

```
Eigenvectors[{{1, 0, 0}, {1, 1, 1}, {1, 2, 4}}]
```

Eliminate   Eliminates variables from a set of simultaneous equations.

```
Eliminate[{x^2 + y + z == 1, x - y + z^2 == 0}, z]
```

Evaluate   Forces evaluation of an expression; often necessary in plotting commands.

```
Plot[Evaluate[Table[i*Exp[x], {i, 0, 20}]],
  {x, -1, 1}]
```

Expand   Expands an algebraic expression.

```
Expand[(x - y)^2]
```

Factor   Factors an expression.

```
Factor[x^100 - y^100]
Factor[x^3 - 2x + 3.0]
Factor[Exp[3x] + Exp[x]]
```

FactorInteger   Finds the prime factorization of a positive integer.

```
FactorInteger[12345678987654321]
```

FindMinimum   Finds the smallest (approximate) value of a function near a given point.

```
FindMinimum[x^3 - 7*x^2 - 5*x + 2, {x, 1}]
```

FindRoot   Finds a numerical solution to an equation near a specified point.

```
FindRoot[Sin[x] == x^2, {x, 1}]
```

First   Selects the first element in a list.

```
First[{a, b, c, d, e}]
First[Solve[x^2 - 1 == 0, x]]
```

Flatten   Removes extra levels of braces in a nested list. An optional integer argument specifies the level of the list at which to flatten.

```
Flatten[Table[f[i, j], {i, 1, 10}, {b, 1, 20}]]
Flatten[{{2}, {4, 6, {8}}, 10}, 1]
```

FullSimplify   Simplifies an expression more completely than **Simplify**.

```
FullSimplify[x*Gamma[x]]
```

Function   Defines a pure function.

```
f = Function[x, Exp[Sqrt[x]] + 1]
```

GraphicsArray   Displays a one- or two-dimensional array of graphics objects.

```
Show[GraphicsArray[{plot1, plot2}]]
```

IdentityMatrix   Produces the identity matrix of a specified size.

```
IdentityMatrix[5] //MatrixForm
```

If   Used for conditional evaluation. If the first argument (the condition) is true, then the second argument is evaluated; otherwise, the third argument is evaluated.

```
f[x_] := If[x != 0, Sin[x]/x, 1]
```

ImplicitPlot   In the **Graphics** package. Plots a curve defined implicitly by an equation.

```
<<Graphics`ImplicitPlot`
ImplicitPlot[x^2 + y^2/4 == 1, {x, -1, 1}]
```

InputForm   Converts Mathematica output into a form suitable for Mathematica input. Sometimes useful for seeing the actual data generated by graphics commands.

```
Plot[Cos[x], {x, -1, 1}] //InputForm
```

Integrate   Computes definite and indefinite integrals.

```
Integrate[x^2*Sin[x], {x, 0, Pi}]   (definite)
Integrate[Exp[-x], x]   (indefinite)
```

Interpolation   Produces a continuous function (which Mathematica calls an **InterpolatingFunction**) from a sequence of (x, y) coordinates by interpolating values.

```
f = Interpolation[{{1, 2}, {3, 8}, {5, 7}}]
Plot[f[x], {x, 1, 5}]
```

Inverse   Finds the inverse of a square matrix.

```
Inverse[{{2.83, 1}, {3, 5}}]
```

InverseLaplaceTransform   In the **Calculus`LaplaceTransform`** package. Computes the inverse Laplace transform.

```
<<Calculus`LaplaceTransform`
InverseLaplaceTransform[1/(s^2 + 1), s, t]
```

Join   Combines two or more lists.

```
Join[{0, 1, 1}, {2, 3, 5}]
```

LabeledListPlot   In the **Graphics`Graphics`** package. Plots a list of points with text labels.

```
<<Graphics`Graphics`
plot1 = Plot[Sin[x], {x, 0, 4 Pi}]
labels = LabeledListPlot[{{Pi/2, 1, "max"},
  {3Pi/2, -1, "min"}}]
Show[{plot1, labels}]
```

LaplaceTransform In the **Calculus`LaplaceTransform`** package. Computes the Laplace transform.

```
<<Calculus`LaplaceTransform`
LaplaceTransform[Cos[t], t, s]
```

Last Selects the last element in a list.

```
Last[Eigensystem[{{1, 2}, {3, 4}}]]
```

Limit Tries to find the limit. By default, the limit is one-sided from the right, except at infinity. To take the limit from the left, use **Direction** –> **1**.

```
Limit[Sin[x]/x, x –> 0]
Limit[Log[x]/x, x –> Infinity]
Limit[Abs[x]/x, x –> 0, Direction –> 1]
```

LinearSolve Solves a linear (matrix) equation. **LinearSolve[A, b]** solves the linear equation $Ax = b$.

```
LinearSolve[{{8, -1}, {1, 1}}, {0, 2}]
```

ListPlot Plots a list of points specified by (x, y)-coordinates.

```
ListPlot[{{1, 1}, {2, 4}, {3, 10}}]
ListPlot[{1, 4, 10}, PlotJoined –> True]
```

Map Applies a function to each element of a list.

```
f[x_] := x^2 + 5x;
Map[f, {1, 2, 3}]
```

MatrixForm Displays output in a rectangular array. Similar to **TableForm**.

```
{{3, 1}, {2, 200}, {4, 5}} //MatrixForm
```

Module Creates reusable program blocks with their own local variables.

```
f[n_] := Module[{a = n, r = 0},
 While[a > 0, r = r + a; a = a - 1]; r]
```

N Gives a numerical (or decimal) approximation of a number with a specified number of digits. The default is 6.

```
N[Pi, 100]
E^2 //N
```

NDSolve Computes numerical solutions for ordinary differential equations.

```
NDSolve[{y´[x] == x^2 + y[x]^2, y[0] == 1},
 y[x], {x, 0, 10}]
```

Nest   Applies a function iteratively to a specified starting value.

```
Nest[Cos, x, 3]
Nest[Cos, Pi/12, 3]
```

NestList   Applies a function iteratively and produces a list of the iterates.

```
NestList[Exp, x, 10]
```

NIntegrate   Carries out numerical integration.

```
NIntegrate[Exp[-x^2], {x, 0, Infinity}]
NIntegrate[x*Log[x], {x, 0, 1}]
```

Normal   Truncates a power series to a polynomial.

```
Normal[Series[Log[1 + x], {x, 0, 8}]]
```

NSolve   Is equivalent to `N[Solve[...]]`.

```
NSolve[x^3 - x^2 + 9 == 0, x]
```

Off   Turns off printing of an error or warning message.

```
Off[Plot::plnr]
```

On   Turns on printing of an error or warning message.

```
On[Plot::plnr]
```

ParametricPlot   Plots one or more curves given by parametric equations.

```
ParametricPlot[{Sin[t], Cos[t]}, {t, 0, 2Pi},
 AspectRatio -> 1]
```

ParametricPlot3D   Draws a space curve or a surface given by parametric equations.

```
ParametricPlot3D[{Cos[t], Sin[t], t}, {t, 0, 4Pi}]
ParametricPlot3D[{(2 + Cos[t])Cos[u], (2 +
 Cos[t])Sin[u], Sin[t]}, {t, 0, 2Pi}, {u, 0, 2Pi}]
```

Part   Extracts one or more elements of a list. For nested lists, extracts elements recursively.

```
Part[{a, b, c, d, e}, {2, 4}]
Part[{{a, b}, {c, d}, e}, 2, 2]
```

PieChart   In the **Graphics`Graphics`** package. Generates a pie chart from the given data.

```
PieChart[{15, 22, 26, 10, 8, 19}, PieLabels ->
 {"Europe", "Africa", "North America",
 "South America", "Asia", "Australia"}]
```

Play   Plays a sound defined by a function.

```
Play[Sin[1000/t], {t, 0, 1}]
```

Plot   Draws a graph of an expression (or list of expressions) of one variable.

```
Plot[Sin[x], {x, 0, 10}]
Plot[{x, x^2, x^3, x^4}, {x, -1, 1}]
```

Plot3D   Draws a graph of an expression of two variables.

```
Plot3D[x^2 - y^2, {x, -1, 1}, {y, -1, 1}]
Plot3D[Cos[x]*y, {x, -10, 10}, {y, -1, 1},
 PlotPoints -> 35]
```

PlotVectorField   In the **Graphics`PlotField`** package. Draws the vector field specified by a pair of expressions in two variables.

```
<<Graphics`PlotField`
PlotVectorField[{y, -x}, {x, -1, 1}, {y, -1, 1},
 AspectRatio -> 1, ScaleFunction -> (1&)]
```

Prime   Returns the nth prime number.

```
Prime[100]
```

Product   Computes the product of successive values of a specified expression.

```
Product[i, {i, 1, 20}]
```

Random   Generates a uniformly distributed (pseudo)random number in the interval $[0, 1]$. The type (**Integer**, **Real**, **Complex**) and range (**{min, max}**) can also be specified.

```
Random[]
Random[Integer, {0, 10}]
```

Remove   Removes symbols completely; useful for removing names of package commands that are mistakenly invoked before the package is loaded.

```
Remove[ImplicitPlot]
```

Roots   Solves a polynomial equation, yielding logical equations instead of the transformation rules returned by **Solve**.

```
Roots[x^2 + 5*x + 6 == 0, x]
```

RSolve   In the **DiscreteMath`RSolve`** package. Solves a recurrence relation symbolically.

```
<<DiscreteMath`RSolve`
RSolve[{a[n + 1] == -2*a[n]/(n + 1), a[0] == 1},
 a[n], n]
```

ScientificForm   Prints a real number in scientific notation.

```
289.423 //ScientificForm
ScientificForm[289.423]
```

Series   Generates terms of a power series expansion about a specified point, up to a specified order.

```
Series[Sin[x], {x, 0, 20}]
```

Short   Restricts the output of a command to one or more lines.

```
Solve[x^10 + 12 == 0, x] //Short
Short[%, 2]
```

Show   Combines and displays one or more previously generated graphics.

```
Show[plot1, plot2]
```

Simplify   Tries to simplify an expression by applying algebraic transformations.

```
Simplify[(x - 1)^(-2) - (x + 1)^(-2)]
(x + 1)^2 - (x^2 - 1) //Simplify
```

Solve   Tries to solve an equation or list of equations exactly.

```
Solve[a*x^2 + b*x + c == 0, x]
Solve[{u + v == 1, -u + 3v == 8}, {u, v}]
```

Sum   Computes the sum of successive values of a specified expression.

```
Sum[i^2, {i, 1, 100}]
Sum[Sin[k], {k, 0, 1, 0.1}]
```

Table   Generates a list by evaluating an expression at successive increments of an index.

```
Table[i, {i, 0, 100}]
Table[{f[j], g[j]}, {j, 0, -1, 1, 0.1}]
```

TableForm   Displays a list in tabular form.

```
Table[{i, Sin[2Pi*i]}, {i, 1, 50}] //TableForm
TableForm[Table[{i, Sin[2Pi*i]}, {i, 1, 50}]]
```

TextListPlot   In the **Graphics`Graphics`** package. Plots a list of points using text symbols. Default is to number each point in order.

```
<<Graphics`Graphics`
TextListPlot[Table[{x, x^2}, {x, 0, 10, 0.5]]
TextListPlot[Table[{x, Log[x], "o"}, {x, 1, 12}]]
```

Transpose   Finds the transpose of a matrix.

```
Transpose[{{a, b}, {c, d}}]
```

Options to Mathematica Commands

AccuracyGoal   Specifies digits of accuracy in a numerical procedure.

```
NDSolve[{y´[x] == x*Exp[y[x]], y[0] == 0}, y[x],
 {x, 0, 2}, WorkingPrecision -> 25,
 PrecisionGoal -> 15, AccuracyGoal -> 15]
```

AspectRatio   Specifies ratio of height to width in a plot. **AspectRatio -> 1** makes the height and width equal. **AspectRatio -> Automatic** instructs Mathematica to use the same scale on each axis.

```
PlotVectorField[{y, -x}, {x, -1, 1}, {y, -1, 1},
 AspectRatio -> 1]
```

Axes   Specifies whether axes should be drawn in a plot.

```
Plot[Sin[t], {t, -3, 3}, Axes -> False]
```

AxesLabel   Specifies labels for axes in a plot.

```
Plot[Sin[t], {t, 0, 2Pi}, AxesLabel ->
 {"time", "angle"}]
```

AxesOrigin   Specifies the point at which the axes cross in a two-dimensional plot.

```
Plot[Sin[x^2] + 1, {x, -2Pi, 2Pi}, AxesOrigin ->
 {0, 1}]
```

Boxed   Specifies whether a box should be drawn around a three-dimensional graphic.

```
Plot3D[Sin[x]*Cos[y], {x, 0, Pi}, {y, 0, Pi},
 Boxed -> False]
```

ClipFill   Controls filling of clipped regions in three-dimensional graphics.

```
Plot3D[10/(x^2 + y^2), {x, -1, 1}, {y, -1, 1},
 ClipFill -> None]
```

Contours   Specifies how many or which level curves to show in a contour plot.

```
ContourPlot[x^2 + y^2, {x, -1, 1}, {y, -1, 1},
 Contours -> {0.5}]
ContourPlot[x^2 + y^2, {x, -1, 1}, {y, -1, 1},
 Contours -> 30]
```

ContourShading   Determines if regions between contours are shaded.

```
ContourPlot[x^2 - y^2, {x, -5, 5}, {y, -5, 5},
 ContourShading -> False]
```

Dashing   Directs that curves should be drawn dashed.

```
ParametricPlot[{Cos[t], Sin[t]}, {t, 0, 2Pi},
 PlotStyle -> Dashing[{0.03}]]
Plot[{Exp[t], t^2}, {t, 0, 2}, PlotStyle ->
 {{}, Dashing[{0.01}]}]
```

Direction   Specifies direction in the **Limit** command. Use **Direction** -> **1** to compute the limit from the left; the default is **Direction** -> **-1**, from the right.

```
Limit[Abs[x]/x, x -> 0, Direction -> 1]
```

Frame   Specifies whether a frame should be drawn around a plot.

```
PlotVectorField[{Sin[x*y], x - y]}, {x, -1, 1},
 {y, 0, 1}, Frame -> True]
```

GrayLevel   Directs that a curve should be plotted in a shade of gray, with 0 representing black and 1 representing white, and numbers in between representing shades between black and white.

```
Plot[Tan[x], {x, 0, Pi/4}, PlotStyle ->
 GrayLevel[0.5]]
Plot[{Cosh[x], Sinh[x]}, {x, 0, 10}, PlotStyle ->
 {{}, GrayLevel[0.6]}]
```

MaxIterations   Specifies maximum number of iterations in commands that use an iterative algorithm. In **FindRoot**, the default is 15.

```
FindRoot[ArcCos[t] == 0.001, {t, 0},
 MaxIterations -> 40]
```

MaxSteps   Specifies maximum number of steps used by **NDSolve**; the default is 1000.

```
NDSolve[{y´´[x] + x*y[x] == 0, y[0] == 1,
 y´[0] == 0}, y[x], {x, 0, 40}, MaxSteps -> 2000]
```

Mesh   Toggles display of the mesh in three-dimensional graphics.

```
Plot3D[x^2 + y^2, {x, -3, 3}, {y, -3, 3}, Mesh ->
 False]
```

PlayRange   Controls the volume of the sound produced by **Play**. Setting the value of **PlayRange** larger than the actual range of the function decreases the volume; setting it smaller increases it.

```
Play[Sin[440t], {t, 0, 10}, PlayRange ->{0, 2}]
```

PlotJoined   Specifies whether to connect the points in a **ListPlot**.

```
ListPlot[{{0, 0}, {1, -3}, {2, 1}}, PlotJoined ->
  True]
```

PlotLabel   Specifies a label for a plot.

```
ListPlot[{7.3, 8.6, 7.1, 6.8, 7.2},
  PlotJoined -> True, PlotLabel -> "Interest Rates"]
```

PlotPoints   Specifies the initial number of sample points for a plot, or the fineness of the grid for contour plots and surface plots. The default is 25 for **Plot**, and 15 for **Plot3D** (specifying a 15×15 grid).

```
Plot[Sin[x^2], {x, 10, 18}, PlotPoints -> 50]
```

PlotRange   Specifies the range of variables in a plot. **PlotRange -> All** shows the full range of the dependent variable. **PlotRange -> Automatic** (the default for most commands) allows clipping of the plot. **PlotRange -> {min, max}** specifies the range for the dependent variable. **PlotRange -> {{xmin, xmax}, {ymin, ymax}}** specifies the ranges of the x and y variables in a two-dimensional plot. **PlotRange -> {{xmin, xmax}, {ymin, ymax}, {zmin, zmax}}** specifies the range of all three variables in a three-dimensional plot.

```
Plot[Tan[x], {x, 0, Pi}, PlotRange -> {0, 10}]
ParametricPlot[{t^3, t^5}, {t, -10, 10},
  PlotRange -> {{-5, 5}, {-10, 10}}]
ContourPlot[x^3 + y^3, {x, -4, 4}, {y, -2, 2},
  PlotRange -> {-100, 100}]
```

PlotStyle   Specifies plotting style of curves or points; *cf.* **GrayLevel**, **Dashing**, **RGBColor**, and **Thickness**.

PrecisionGoal   A numerical precision option; *cf.* **AccuracyGoal**.

RGBColor   Directs that a curve should be plotted in a color specified by levels of red, green, and blue.

```
Plot[Tan[x], {x, 0, Pi/4}, PlotStyle ->
  RGBColor[1, 0.5, 0]]
```

ScaleFunction   Used for scaling vectors in vector field plots.

```
PlotVectorField[{f[x, y], g[x, y]}, {x, -1, 1},
  {y, -2, 2}, ScaleFunction -> (1&)]
```

Shading Toggles shading of surfaces in three-dimensional graphics.

```
Plot3D[Sin[x] Cos[y], {x, 0, 4*Pi}, {y, 0, 4*Pi},
  Shading -> False]
```

TableHeadings Puts labels on the rows and columns of tables or matrices.

```
TableForm[Table[{x, x^2}, {x, 1, 4}],
  TableHeadings -> {None, {"Numbers", "Squares"}}]
```

Thickness Directs that a curve should be plotted at a specified thickness.

```
Plot[{Sin[x], Cos[x]}, PlotStyle ->
  {{}, Thickness[0.01]}]
```

Ticks Specifies tick marks for the axes in a plot. The following example sets ticks at 0, 0.5, and 1 on the x-axis and directs Mathematica to set them "automatically" on the y-axis.

```
Plot[x^2, {x, -1, 1}, Ticks -> {{0, 0.5, 1},
  Automatic}]
```

ViewPoint Specifies the viewpoint for three-dimensional graphics.

```
Plot3D[Cos[x]*y, {x, -10, 10}, {y, -1, 1},
  PlotPoints -> 35, ViewPoint -> {0, -1, 0}]
```

WorkingPrecision Specifies how many digits of precision should be maintained internally during certain numerical procedures; *cf.* **AccuracyGoal**.

Built-in Functions

Abs The absolute value function, $|x|$.

ArcCos The arccosine (inverse cosine) function.

ArcSin The arcsine (inverse sine) function.

ArcTan The arctangent (inverse tangent) function.

Arg Gives the argument (angle) of a complex number.

```
Arg[1 - Sqrt[3]*I]
```

Conjugate Gives the complex conjugate of a complex number.

```
Conjugate[1 - 5*I]
```

Cos The cosine function.

Cosh   The hyperbolic cosine function.

Erf   The *error function* $\operatorname{erf}(x) = (2/\sqrt{\pi}) \int_0^x e^{-t^2}\, dt$.

Erfi   The imaginary error function, $-i\operatorname{erf}(ix)$.

Exp   The exponential function, e^x.

Factorial   The factorial of an integer, $n!$.

Im   The imaginary part of a complex number, $\operatorname{Im}(z)$.

Log   The natural logarithm, $\ln x = \log_e x$.

Max   Returns the maximum element of a list of numbers.

```
Max[{1, 8, 7, 4}]
```

Min   Returns the minimum element of a list of numbers.

Re   The real part of a complex number, $\operatorname{Re}(z)$.

Round   Rounds a number to the closest integer.

Sign   Returns $-1, 0$, or 1, depending on whether the argument is negative, zero, or positive.

Sin   The sine function.

Sinh   The hyperbolic sine function.

Sqrt   The square root function.

Tan   The tangent function.

Tanh   The hyperbolic tangent function.

Built-in Constants

Degree $\pi/180$, the number of radians in 1 degree. To convert from radians to degrees, multiply by **Degree**.

E $e = \ln^{-1}(1)$.

GoldenRatio   The Golden Ratio, $(1 + \sqrt{5})/2$.

I   The complex number $i = \sqrt{-1}$.

Infinity ∞ (infinity).

Pi π.

Some Standard Packages

Algebra`InequalitySolve`   Contains a command to solve inequalities.

Calculus`FourierTransform`   Contains several procedures for working with Fourier transforms.

Calculus`LaplaceTransform`   Contains several procedures for working with Laplace transforms.

Calculus`VectorAnalysis`   Contains procedures needed for multivariable calculus, including **Div**, **Grad**, and **Curl**.

DiscreteMath`Combinatorica`   Contains functions useful in combinatorics and graph theory.

DiscreteMath`RSolve`   Contains several procedures, such as **RSolve** and **GeneratingFunction**, to study recurrence relations.

Graphics`Animation`   Contains procedures to simplify the creation of animations.

Graphics`ContourPlot3D`   Contains the **ContourPlot3D** command.

Graphics`Graphics`   Contains many specialized graphing commands, including **BarChart**, **PieChart**, **LogPlot**, and **PolarPlot**.

Graphics`Graphics3D`   Contains several specialized commands for producing three-dimensional graphics, including **BarChart3D** and **Shadow**.

Graphics`ImplicitPlot`   Contains the **ImplicitPlot** command.

Graphics`PlotField`   Contains commands to plot vector fields.

Miscellaneous`ChemicalElements`   Contains commands that read information from the periodic table.

Statistics`ConfidenceIntervals`   Contains commands to calculate confidence intervals for various statistics.

Statistics`DescriptiveStatistics`   Contains commands such as **Mean**, **Mode**, and **Variance** that calculate various statistics of data sets.

Statistics`HypothesisTests`   Contains commands for performing hypothesis tests on data sets.

Index

The index uses the same conventions for fonts that are used throughout the book. Mathematica commands, such as **DSolve**, are printed in a boldface typewriter font. Menu options, such as **File**, are printed in boldface. Everything else is printed in a standard font.